Let's Explore...

The British Isles

Educator Reviews for
Let's Explore the British Isles

Fens, fells, drumlins, and downs. Caroline Walker claims, "geography is about the way places shape the lives of the people who live there" and it would be hard to find a more engaging child's introduction to the geography of the British Isles than the beautiful and brilliant one she shares. Guided by a warm knowledgeable storyteller—with nary a list of definitions, chart of facts, or set of questions to answer—the reader leaves on an imaginary journey to, around, and through the United Kingdom and the Republic of Ireland aided only by the conversational literary style of the storyteller, increasingly detailed watercolour maps, and artistic photographs, each element adding to the majesty and memorability of the story told. One can imagine that while reading through this geography, a student will eagerly reach for one of the novels noted, Swallows and Amazons or Wind in the Willows perhaps, search to learn more about King Arthur, the Spanish Armada, William the Conqueror, Captain James Cook, Shakespeare's Macbeth, the meadows of Runnymede or the forests of Nottingham, or even seek a recipe to make parkin. The ease with which Walker situates numerous historical, cultural, literary, and religious figures into a geography work for young children is masterful. Her gentle expansive work, in addition to finding a place on the shelves of all discerning homeschools and classrooms across the world, might most naturally find its home on the bedside table of a child enchanted by stories and adventures.

> **- Reviewed by Deani Van Pelt, PhD**
> Ancaster, Ontario, Canada
> Charlotte Mason Institute

'If geography is God's artistry writ large upon the earth, then our responses should be ones of joy and wonder before His Providence, power, and creativity. Charlotte Mason venerated those very works God inscribed upon His created order and desired that children should experience the diversity and beauty of the world around them. Here is a book that unfolds a well-told story of the spaces and places that are the British Isles. Well-written prose combines with delightful illustrations to offer the reader's mind and imagination a feast of fertile ideas.'

- Dr. Jack Edward Beckman (Cantab)
Professor of Education, Covenant College

The reader journeys with the traveler from land to sea and back again, receiving ideas of the rich history of places and persons in conjunction with delightful illustrations of maps and images throughout the British Isles.

- Maryellen St. Cyr,
Founder of Ambleside Schools International

'Well written, age-appropriate narrative texts play a central role in our Charlotte Mason inspired curriculum. We find that attentive listening to an uninterrupted reading followed by narration helps children get in touch with knowledge -- in this case about the British Isles -- in uniquely effective ways. Read this text and I am sure you too will make many fresh discoveries! I am delighted to see this groundbreaking publication of Let's Explore the British Isles by Caroline Walker and hope teachers around the world will find it as valuable a classroom tool as we do.'

- Jason Fletcher
Headmaster, Heritage School, Cambridge

In the preface of book V of Charlotte Mason's Geography books on the Old and New World 1908, is the following statement: *"the author has tried to bring before the reader vivid pictures of the regions treated of, and familiar ideas as to the manner of life of the people who dwell in those regions. Further than this, her aim has been to furnish such interesting and attractive matter as should further the fascinating study of geography."*

Mason goes on to say that her book's absence of pictures is of little consequence, *"since we all know that the pictures which abide with us are those which the imagination constructs from written or spoken descriptions".*

Delightfully Caroline Walker's book doesn't choose one or the other, but provides both: effectively descriptive language through verbal illustrations that allow us to imagine the beauty and climate and spectacular contrast of the terrain of the British Isles, while at the same time sharing beautiful photographs and colorful illustrations of these isles that are timely and necessary for today's schooling and home education.

I particularly enjoyed her use of placing a fictitious child in the different geographic settings, to let the students better understand the variations in lifestyles of the families in each region, being able to place themselves within that locale. This practice is particularly important as the students in other countries can then picture themselves in a vibrant environment far different perhaps from their own.

In my view, the content contained in this narrative can rightfully be called a living book, one which feeds the children with information that is nourishing and pleasing to their study, their eyes, and their imaginations.

- **Bobby Scott,**
M.Ed Counseling; M.Ed. School Administration
Headmaster Emeritus Perimeter School, 1986-2020
Director, ChildLight Schools

"I have been using this wonderful book with my Year 4 class (8 and 9 year olds) as part of our Geography studies on the British Isles. The children have responded really well to the narrative style (it is much more engaging than a dry text book) and the pictures are inspiring too. The book covers both physical geographical information as well as some interesting details on cities and regions. It also makes reference to some historical details which helps the children to see the connections between, for example, their learning about the Anglo-Saxons and the development of regions. The book has certainly been a welcome addition to my teaching resources."
- **Helen Eldridge,**
Teacher at Heritage School, Cambridge.

One of the biggest challenges to educators practicing Charlotte Mason's methods today is the difficulty in finding books that are factually up-to-date and culturally relevant and that are written using literary narrative, as opposed to snippets and side-bars. This book answers with current information and engaging vignettes written in the style of Mason's The Forty Shires.
- **Jennifer Spencer, EdD**
Visiting Research Fellow, University of Cumbria

This edition published 2023
by Living Book Press

ISBN: 978-1-922919-11-3   (hardcover)
        978-1-922919-10-6 (softcover)

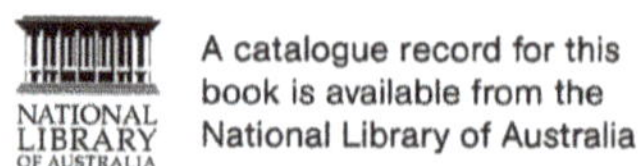

A catalogue record for this book is available from the National Library of Australia

Let's Explore
The British Isles

Written by

CAROLINE WALKER

Maps and illustrations by

GLORIS SMITH YOUNG

with map typography by

ANDREA FORCE

LIVING BOOK
PRESS

Regions

Introduction
FOR PARENTS AND TEACHERS

In her educational philosophy, Charlotte Mason didn't want children just to be seen as receptacles for facts, but rather for them to truly engage with the world and in the process, own their knowledge and understanding for themselves. One key to this, she thought, was appealing to children's imagination, particularly through stories, and this is the thinking behind this book, Let's Explore the British Isles. Unlike some current books that focus on facts, figures, charts and photographs, this book seeks to talk about the geography of the British Isles as a narrative, giving the reader a sense of being there, along with the illustrations of maps, pictures and photos.

As such, it can be read individually or read out loud to a class. To assist children to engage with their material, Mason encouraged them to pay careful attention to what they read or heard and then tell back what they remembered. This narration approach to learning can be very helpful.

As a children's book it tries to give only the most salient and relevant geographical information, but it does so in places with some historical context where that has real value. The maps are there to illustrate the text rather than be too detailed. For example, not all the counties of Ireland are included and none are shown for Scotland and Wales. If you live in the British Isles, we hope this book will help you to explore and know them more and if you live elsewhere, that you will be able to visit and enjoy them too.

Contents

1.   Where To Find the British Isles   1
2.   The Countries of the British Isles   7
3.   The Landforms of the British Isles   11
4.   The Water Features of the British Isles   17
5.   The Coast of the British Isles - part 1   23
6.   The Coast of the British Isles - part 2   31
7.   The Islands of the British Isles   37
8.   The Cities of the British Isles   43
9.   London   49
10. South East England   55
11. South West England   61
12. The West Midlands   67
13. The East Midlands   73
14. East Anglia   79
15. Yorkshire   85
16. North West England   91
17. North East England   97
18. Scotland - the Lowlands   103
19. Scotland - the Highlands   111
20. Wales   117
21. Northern Ireland   125
22. Republic of Ireland - part 1   131
23. Republic of Ireland - part 2   136
24. Conclusion   141

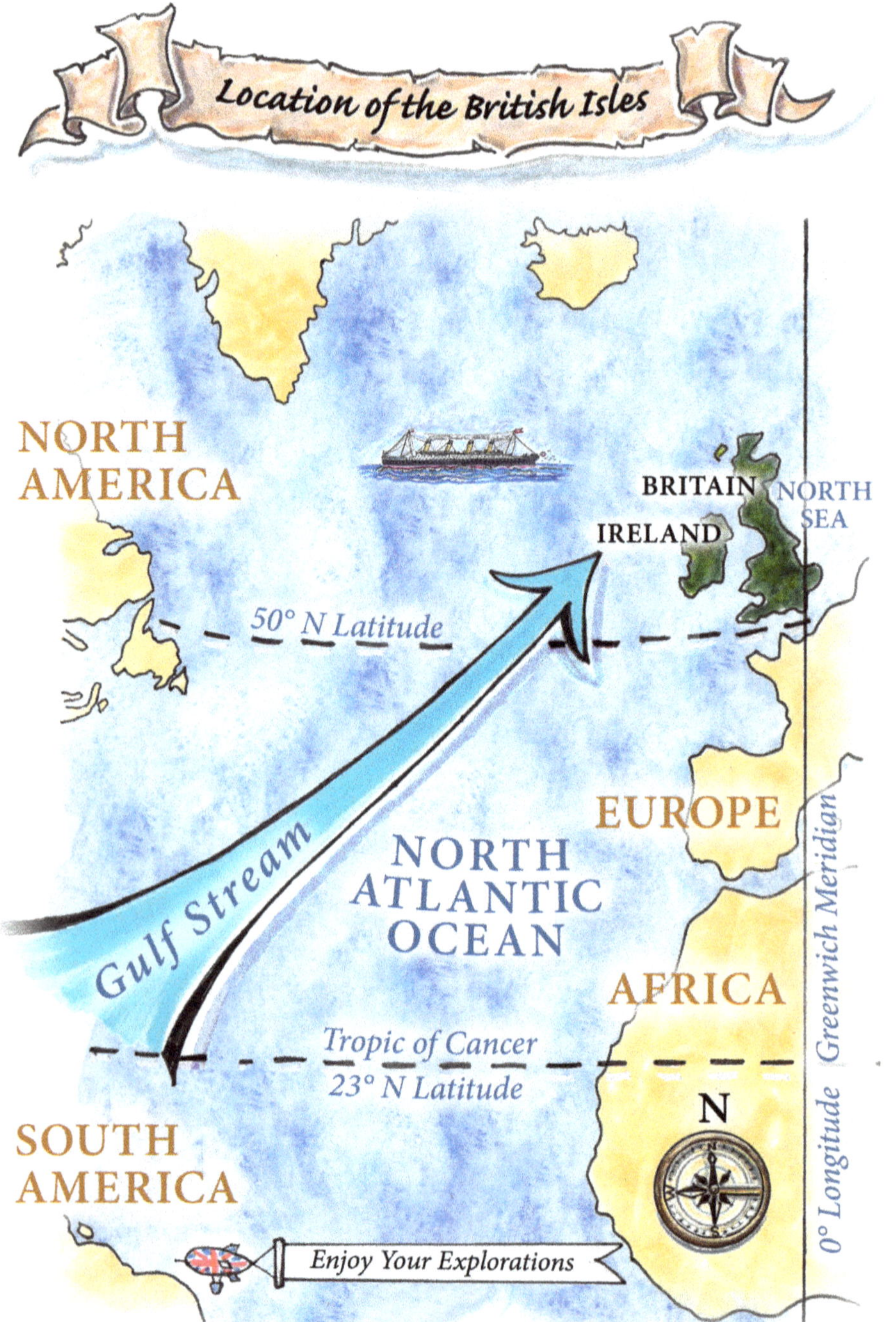

Location of the British Isles
NORTH AMERICA
BRITAIN
IRELAND
NORTH SEA
50° N Latitude
Gulf Stream
EUROPE
NORTH ATLANTIC OCEAN
AFRICA
Tropic of Cancer
23° N Latitude
N
SOUTH AMERICA
0° Longitude Greenwich Meridian
Enjoy Your Explorations

chapter 1

Where To Find the British Isles

THE FIRST THING we must find out about the British Isles is exactly where in the world they are. Look at a globe or a map of the whole world. Find the Atlantic Ocean, which is a vast expanse of waves and water. North of the Equator it is called the North Atlantic Ocean, and you will see on its western shore the continent of North America. On the eastern side you can find part of Africa and, further north, the continent of Europe. Keep your eyes travelling northwards across Europe and you will find two islands just off its north-western coast, one larger, one smaller. Now you have found the British Isles. You will see that to the south and east of the British Isles is continental Europe, and to the west is the North Atlantic Ocean. If you were to travel still further north, you would find the Arctic Circle and, eventually, the North Pole itself.

On most maps of the world, you can only see these two islands of the British Isles. The larger island is called Great Britain and the smaller is called Ireland. If you were to zoom closer, however, you would find that these two larger islands are surrounded by thousands of smaller islands. Some examples are Anglesey, the Isle of Man, the Isle of Wight, the Channel Islands, the Isles of Scilly and off Scotland, the Hebrides, Orkneys and Shetlands. Altogether, with Great Britain and Ireland, these thousands of islands are known as the British Isles.

Like all islands, the British Isles are surrounded by water. As we have already seen, to the west there is the mighty North Atlantic Ocean. The sea off the eastern coast of Great Britain is called, not the east sea, but the North Sea, as it lies to the north of much of Europe. Moving further south, the stretch of sea which separates England from France (which is on mainland Europe) is called the English Channel. The very narrowest

SATELLITE MAP OF THE BRITISH ISLES

section of the English Channel is called the Strait of Dover, where the English town of Dover is just 20 miles away from the French town of Calais. The sea which lies between Great Britain and Ireland is known as the Irish Sea.

The British Isles, like all of Europe, are in the Northern Hemisphere. This means they are north of the Equator, indeed north of the Tropic of Cancer, and relatively close to the North Pole. You can use a measure called latitude to describe how far north or south a place is. The starting line is the Equator, at 0 degrees, the furthest north you can go is the North Pole, at 90 degrees. The British Isles are found between 50 and 60 degrees North. Other lands at this latitude, in Canada and Russia have very hot summers and freezing winters. The British Isles, by contrast, have a mild climate, with warm or cool temperatures and plenty of rain and overcast weather all through the year. This is because the Atlantic Ocean, with its warm current called the Gulf Stream, brings relatively warm water and air to its shores and keeps the temperature fairly moderate. The name of this type of climate is called temperate maritime. Temperate means it is not extreme, and maritime means it is by the sea.

You can describe how far east or west a place is by using

lines of longitude. The invisible starting line for longitude, at 0 degrees is called the Prime Meridian, and the special thing about this is that it runs right through the British Isles! In fact, the 0 degree line is often called the Greenwich Meridian, named after Greenwich, which is in London. This is because Greenwich had a Royal Observatory, where a great telescope helped people study the position of the stars, and work out their longitude. So, the British Isles range from 1 degree East to 10 degrees West, and if you go to Greenwich you can stand with one foot in the Eastern Hemisphere and one foot in the Western Hemisphere.

THE PRIME MERIDIAN.

Buenos Aires 5
Montevideo 5
Town 18 2
Canberra 149°
Wellington 174°
Hobart 147° 18 E

Countries of the British Isles
Nessie is holding the Union Jack which is the flag of the United Kingdom, but not Ireland.
NORTH SEA
Scottish
SCOTLAND
Edinburgh
Imperial State Crown
NORTHERN IRELAND
Belfast
Dublin
IRELAND (EIRE)
Irish
Welsh
WALES
Cardiff
ENGLAND
English
London
ATLANTIC OCEAN
FRANCE

chapter 2

The Countries of the British Isles.

THE BRITISH ISLES, as we have found, are formed from many thousand islands, but they all belong to just two countries: the United Kingdom and the Republic of Ireland. These may be just two countries, but they have quite a complicated story, so we'll have to concentrate! Let us start with the island of Great Britain. Great Britain, as we have seen, is the largest island of the British Isles. Its name comes from 'Britannia,' the name for most of the island during the days of the Roman Empire. It is called 'great' because it is the biggest island. Within the island of Great Britain there are three distinct nations, called England, Scotland and Wales. England is the biggest with by far the largest population of 56 million, and is in the south and east of Great Britain. Scotland is in the north with 5 and a half million and Wales is the smallest with just over 3 million and lies to the west of England. An easy way to remember this is that Wales starts with 'W' for 'west'. So England, Scotland and Wales are together on the island of Great Britain.

Many hundreds of years ago, England, Scotland and Wales were all separate kingdoms, independent from each other, with their own kings, customs and even languages. But over hundreds of years of history, including armed invasions, royal marriages, new laws and popular agreements, all three nations have been joined together into one country. Most laws governing Britain are made by the central government, based in Westminster in London, the capital city of England. Scotland and Wales also have local parliaments in their capital cities of Edinburgh and Cardiff, which make laws about matters such as health, education, taxation and the economy.

Now we look at the island of Ireland. In the northern part of Ireland there is a region called Northern Ireland with a population of nearly 2 million. Its capital city is called Belfast. Although Northern Ireland is separated from Great Britain by the Irish Sea, it is joined, or united, to Great Britain in its government. In this way, Northern Ireland is united with the nations of England, Scotland and Wales, in one, united, kingdom. This may sound complicated, but the best way to remember how these nations are related to one another is to remember the country's name: the United Kingdom. Known as the UK for short, its full name is the United Kingdom of Great Britain and Northern Ireland. When you recall that Great Britain is made up of England, Scotland and Wales, this name helps us see that the United Kingdom of Great Britain and Northern Ireland is a union of four parts: England, Scotland, Wales and Northern Ireland. The Union Flag incorporates the colours and crosses of each national flag, and everyone in the United Kingdom uses the same type of money, or currency. The currency is called pounds, and every coin and note has a picture of the monarch.

So far we have found out about the three nations of Great Britain and the fact that they are joined with the northern part of Ireland, Northern Ireland. But what about the southern, larger part of Ireland? This is a separate country altogether, a sovereign state called Ireland or Éire. It is often called the Republic of Ireland, to distinguish it from Northern Ireland. The Republic of Ireland has its own laws and currency, separate to the United Kingdom, and its people are Irish, not British and there are nearly 5 million of them. The money is the Euro as the Republic is part of the European Union, and each coin and note has a picture of the many European countries which use it. The Republic of Ireland is called a republic, not a kingdom, because its government is led by a president, not a king or queen. Ireland has its own parliament, called the Oireachtas, which meets and makes laws in its capital city, Dublin.

FLAG OF ENGLAND

FLAG OF SCOTLAND

FLAG OF WALES

FLAG OF THE
UNITED KINGDOM

FLAG OF IRELAND

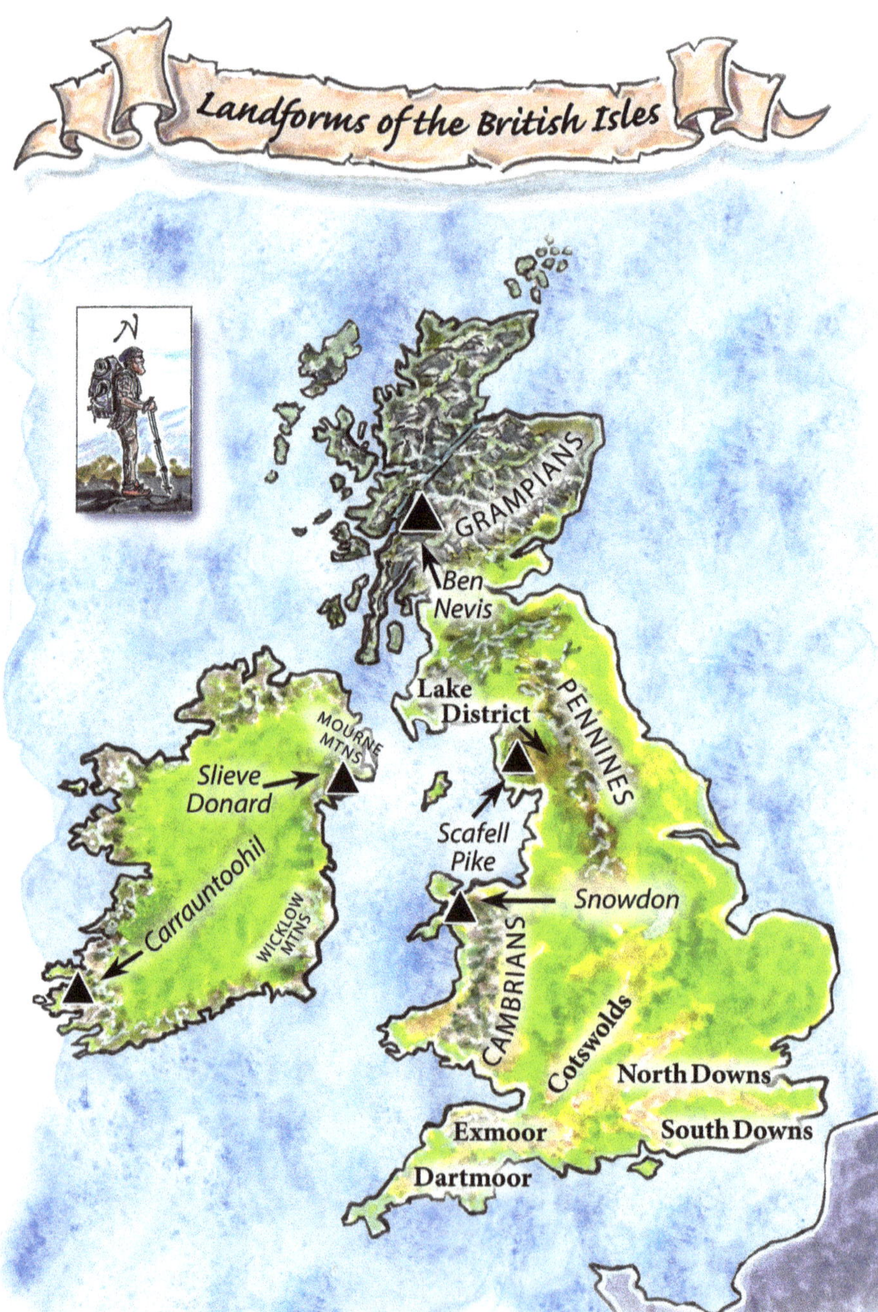

Landforms of the British Isles
N
GRAMPIANS
Ben Nevis
Lake District
PENNINES
MOURNE MTNS
Slieve Donard
Scafell Pike
Snowdon
Carrauntoohil
WICKLOW MTNS
CAMBRIANS
Cotswolds
North Downs
South Downs
Exmoor
Dartmoor

chapter 3

The Landforms of the British Isles

THE MOUNTAINS, HILLS AND LOWLANDS

THE LANDSCAPE OF the British Isles varies greatly, from mountainous peaks, rugged coastlines, gently rolling hills and flat meadows and fens. Let us start with the loftiest heights and work our way down to the lowest plains. Roughly speaking, that journey will also take us from Great Britain's north-west to south-east, from the mountains of Scotland and Wales to flatter lands of south-east England. Then in Ireland we will climb from the low central plain to the mountainous coastline all around. But, let us begin in the north, in Scotland.

The Grampian mountains are a mighty range of giants, formed of ancient hard granite, which dominate the landscape of northern Scotland. Their tallest mountain, which is also the highest peak of the British Isles, is an extinct volcano called Ben Nevis. This giant stands at 1,345 metres and its name can mean 'mountain with its head in the clouds' or 'venomous mountain'! Compared to the world's loftiest mountain ranges, these mountains are small. We can contrast Ben Nevis (1,345 metres) with the highest mountain in Western Europe (Mont Blanc, at 4,809 metres) and the highest mountain in the world

(Mount Everest, at an astonishing 8,848 metres). Nevertheless, to walk among the great peaks and deep glens is to lose oneself in the beautiful grandeur and drama of the Highlands, where majestic red deer roam and golden eagles soar. This is also the land of the clever ptarmigan and mountain hare, whose feathers and fur turn white in the winter to camouflage against the snow. This snow lies thickly on the mountaintops for several months a year and, in some places, it never melts at all.

Wales is similarly a land dominated by mountains and valleys. The Cambrian mountains are formed of high windswept plateaus covered with rough moorland plants and dotted with small lakes. These are separated by narrow valleys with steep sides and picturesque waterfalls. Further north, the highest peak in Wales is Mount Snowdon, whose name means 'snow hill', which stands at 1,085 metres. This pyramid-shaped mountain has a jagged peak which you could climb on a 6-8 hour hike or a pleasant trip on the Snowdon Mountain Railway! On its slopes you will find wild goats, alpine flowers and choughs—crows with red beaks and feet.

The highest mountain in England is called Scafell Pike, which is 978m tall and can be found among several similar giants in the Lake District in north-west England. The principal range of hills in England are the Pennines, which form something of a backbone running down the middle of northern England. Perhaps you can feel your own backbone, or spine, running down from your neck to the centre of your back. England's backbone is made of rocks called limestone and millstone grit. The great high hills are flat and bleak at the top, and largely covered in moorland and patches of exposed rock. Between these wide high hills are beautiful sheltered valleys, such as the Yorkshire Dales.

Southern England is chiefly covered in a landscape of gently rolling hills. The North and South Downs, for example, are hills in South East England. Even though 'downs' sound like they are low down, they are actually 'ups', hills! They are formed from layers of softer sedimentary rock, such as white chalk, and covered by grassland and fields of crops. On a pleasant walk along a chalky path you could see that this is an ideal habitat for butterflies and wildflowers including some rare orchids. These chalk hills typically have a steep slope on one side, called an 'escarpment', and on the other side there is a more gentle, 'dip' slope, which shows the gentle angle of the layers of rock that are lying beneath the fields. Further west, the Cotswolds are hills formed from yellow-coloured limestone, which is quarried and used to build the stone houses in its pretty villages.

In parts of South West England, the landscape looks more rugged and dramatic, from the craggy cliffs of Cornwall to the high moorland of Dartmoor and Exmoor. Here, deep in the ground, sedimentary rocks and granite have been heated and pressed together over time. This has created special types of rock called ores, which contain tiny pieces of metal minerals. Thousands of years ago, people realised that if they mined, or dug up, and heated these metal ores, they could extract the useful metal. The metal could be made into tools, plates and all sorts of other things. The most common metal ores mined here were copper, tin, silver and arsenic, and from the Bronze Age to the late twentieth century, metals from South West England were used and traded throughout the country and overseas.

In Ireland there is a central low-lying plain, scattered with lakes, peat bogs and marshes. Here and there on the flat land are distinct oval-shaped hills called drumlins, which are thought to have been created at the end of the last ice age. This large plain is surrounded by high hills and mountains on almost every side,

THE ROLLING HILLS OF THE COTSWOLDS

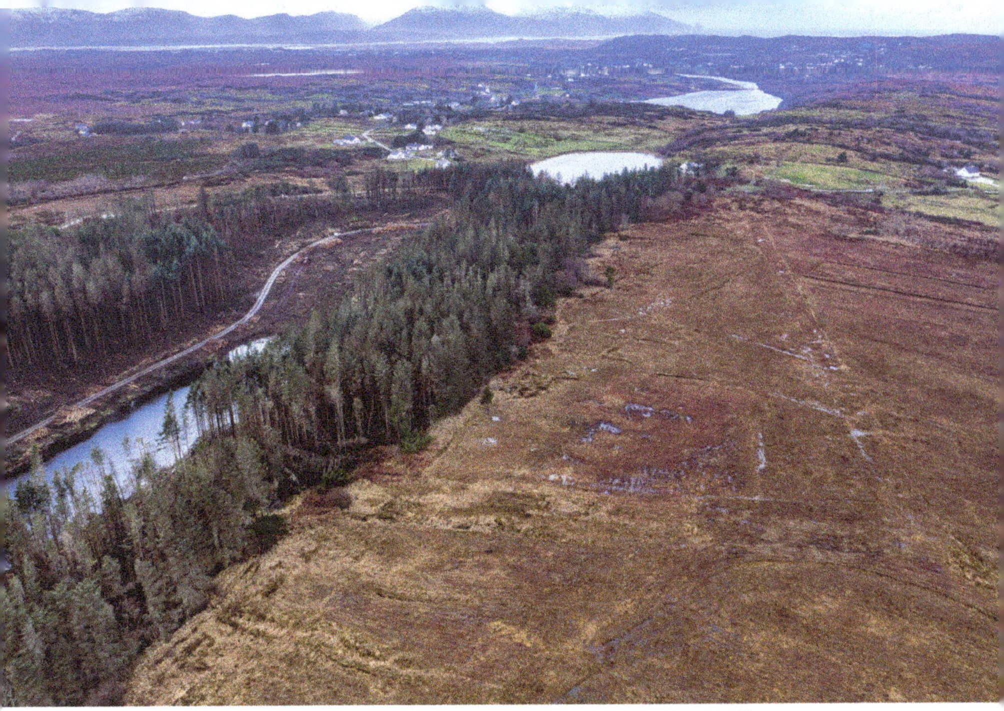

Peat bogs and marshes in Ireland

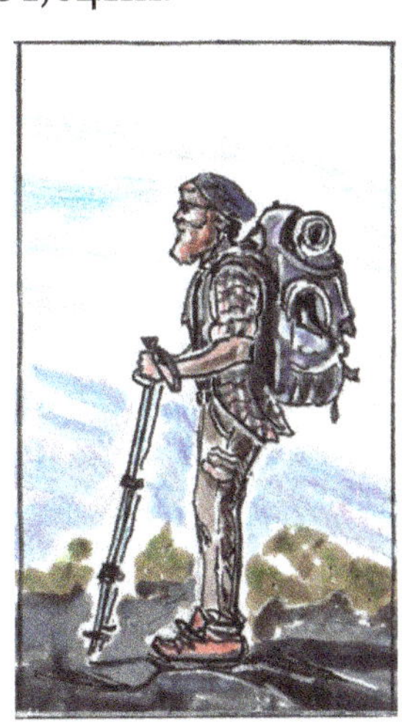

which create some dramatic coastal scenery. Northern Ireland's highest mountains, the granite Mourne Mountains, stand majestically near the sea where the highest peak, Slieve Donard, rises 850m above the waves. At the opposite side of the island, in the south-west, a range of lofty sandstone mountains called the Macgillycuddy Reeks are the highest in all Ireland, and their champion, Carrauntoohil, reaches 1,041m.

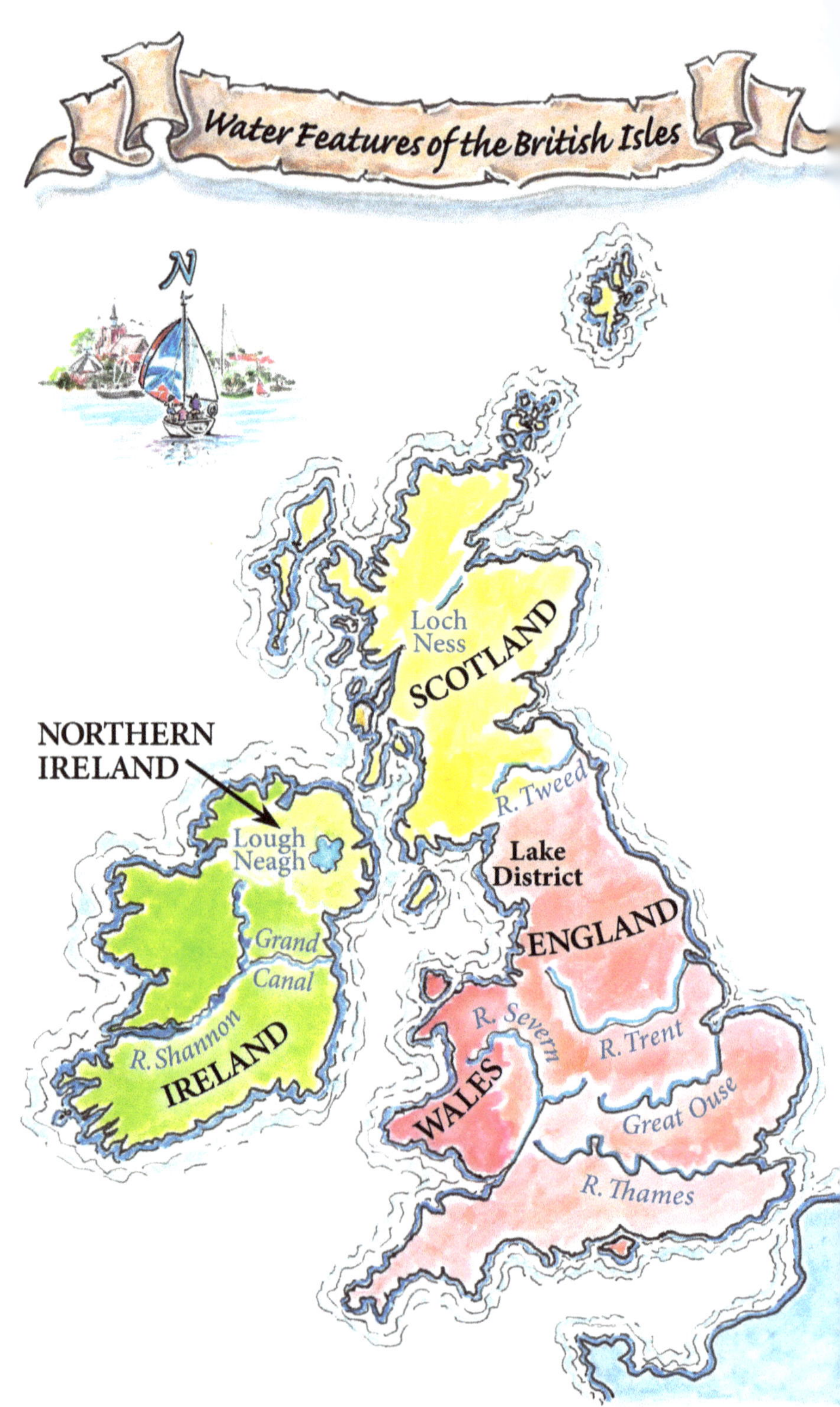

Water Features of the British Isles
N
Loch Ness
SCOTLAND
NORTHERN IRELAND
Lough Neagh
R. Tweed
Lake District
ENGLAND
Grand Canal
R. Shannon
IRELAND
R. Severn
WALES
R. Trent
Great Ouse
R. Thames

chapter 4

The Water Features of the British Isles

THE RIVERS, CANALS AND LAKES

WE HAVE ALREADY noticed the seas that surround the British Isles. Within the isles themselves there are large expanses of freshwater, known as lakes in England, lochs in Scotland, llyns in Wales and loughs in Ireland. By far the largest is Lough Neagh in Northern Ireland, which can be clearly seen on a map of the whole country and is surrounded by flat grassland and bogland. Next in size are the many Scottish lochs, nestled dramatically between highland mountains. The most famous is Loch Ness, known for its fabled monster, 'Nessie', and its remarkable size. Although the surface area of Loch Lomond is bigger, Loch Ness is long and very deep, nearly 40 km long and deeper than the North Sea. In fact, there is more water in Loch Ness than in all the lakes of England and Wales put together!

Nevertheless, there are some large and beautiful lakes, particularly in the area known as the Lake District in north-west England. Perhaps you have read William Wordsworth's poetry, Beatrix Potter's tales of animals, or Arthur Ransome's

Swallows and Amazons? All of these were inspired by the high hills, blue waters and charming wildlife of the Lake District. There are also many reservoirs in the British Isles, which are man-made lakes, created to provide drinking water for millions of people living in nearby cities. They are usually made by building dams in rivers or lakes, but they are designed to look as natural as possible and are often very good habitats for wildlife. Some people enjoy fishing or sailing around reservoirs, and sometimes the water is used to generate power. This type of power, called hydroelectric power, is created by the force of water gushing down pipes or through dams and turning great turbines, to generate electricity. This might then be used in people's homes when they switch on the lights or boil the kettle. Hydroelectric power or HEP is similar in principle to the dynamos on some bikes, which use the movement of the wheels to generate electricity to power the bike's headlights.

There are many rivers and streams, which flow across every part of the land. Some pass rapidly through rocky gullies and fall as gushing waterfalls, particularly over the ancient rocks of Scotland, northern England and Wales. Further south, sedate rivers meander slowly between flat meadows. Some converge on their way to the sea, to create wide estuaries that are crossed by bridges more than a mile long. Fast or slow, water, as you know, always seeks the lowest place it can reach, and these rivers finally reach the sea, whether to the north, east, south or west. There are many long and important rivers, but two of the principal rivers in Great Britain are the Severn and Thames. Water from streams and rivers across Wales and central England join the River Severn on its 220 mile journey to the sea. We see how they gush through a gorge, then pass serenely through gentle valleys, until they finally join the sea at a vast muddy estuary that separates England from Wales. The 215 mile River Thames begins as a trickle in the Cotswold hills and is known as the Isis until it reaches Oxford. The river meanders peacefully through gentle vales, and many rowers and pleasure boats enjoy its calm waters. It flows in an easterly direction passing through the great capital city, London, and then out into the North Sea.

THE SEVERN BRIDGE CROSSING NEAR THE MOUTH OF THE RIVER SEVERN

In its estuary a huge flood barrier has been built to prevent high tides from flooding London.

In Ireland, the longest river is the mighty River Shannon, named after a Celtic goddess called Sionnnan. The river's source is a small pool known as the Shannon Pot in County Cavan, towards the north of Ireland. Its water is slow, shallow and clean, and ideal for fishing and boating. The Shannon flows through several lakes, beside many bogs and marshes, through the historic city of Limerick and along a 70 mile estuary before finally entering the Atlantic Ocean to the west of Ireland. The River Shannon is connected to Dublin, the Irish capital city, by two man-made rivers, or canals, called the Grand Canal and the Royal Canal. There is also a substantial network of canals across central and northern England. These were built in the days before railways, and long before cars or aeroplanes had been invented. On the canals, barges carried coal, iron and heavy goods to and from factories and cities during the Industrial Revolution. Now the traffic on canals is mostly quaint narrowboats. Some people take holidays on narrowboats, while others call them home.

RIVERBOAT ON A CANAL

THE SHANNON POT, START OF THE RIVER SHANNON

Coast of the British Isles
September 1588: Spanish Armada in Atlantic storms
Cape Wrath
John o'Groats
Peterhead
Aberdeen
SCOTLAND
Firth of Tay
Firth of Forth
Glasgow
Edinburgh
ATLANTIC OCEAN
NORTH SEA
NORTHERN IRELAND
Belfast
Whitby
The Humb
Wild Atlantic Way
Morecambe Bay
ENGLAND
Dublin
Liverpool
IRELAND
King's Lynn
IRISH SEA
WALES
Dunwich
London
Tilbur
Cardiff
Bristol
Southampton
Portsmouth
Plymouth
Brixham
Land's End
Strait of Dover
English Channel
FRANCE
July 1588: Spanish Armada enters the English Channel

chapter 5

The Coast of the British Isles

THE CLIFFS, BEACHES AND ESTUARIES – PART I

THE COAST IS where the land meets the sea. Of course, the British Isles are islands surrounded by the sea, so there is a lot of coast! Imagine walking all the way around it, you would walk several thousand miles, and it would take you years! Go to any place in the whole of the British Isles and you will never be more than 70 miles, or a couple of hours' car journey, from the sea. The coast might be steep cliffs, sandy dunes or flat banks of shingle, depending on the type of rock, and the way in which the land has been shaped by rivers and seas over the centuries. In a similar way, the people of these island nations have been shaped by the sea and the opportunities it gives for exploring, trading, invading, fishing and having fun at the beach.

Let us take a tour of the coastline, starting at the tip of Cornwall in the far south-west of England, at a point called Land's End. This land is a peninsula, which means it has water surrounding it on three sides. The Cornish coastline is extremely rocky and craggy. Steep granite cliffs jut into the sea and powerful waves crash around rocks and reefs. As we (carefully!) sail eastwards towards the English Channel we find that, nestled between the cliff headlands, there are coves and creeks which at one time sheltered many smugglers. Small towns keep their fishing boats in harbours protected by thick sea walls, and one town has such a tiny gap between its harbour walls that it is called Mousehole.

Sailing on we start to retrace the route of the ill-fated Spanish Armada, a great fleet of galleons sent by the Catholic King Philip II of Spain to overthrow the Protestant Queen Elizabeth I of England. As the Armada passed the Devon town of Plymouth in July 1588, Sir Francis Drake is said to have finished his game of bowls before setting out with his own fleet into the English Channel. Beacons were lit all along the south coast of England to warn people that the Spanish were coming. Following their route, we pass a pretty crescent called Tor Bay, which faces east and so is sheltered from the fierce south-westerly winds and waves of the Atlantic Ocean. In this bay there is a small town called Brixham, whose houses, like many traditional harbour towns, are painted blue, white and pink. One hundred years after the Spanish Armada sailed past, the people of Brixham witnessed a successful invasion, the 'Glorious Revolution' of 1688, in which the British King James II was replaced by his daughter Mary and her husband, William of Orange. It was also here in Brixham that fishermen first used a technique called trawling, which involves pulling a net through the water behind a boat. Now this method is used all over the world, for many kinds of fish, and around the British coastline trawlers catch mackerel and cod. 'Bottom trawling', however, where the net

is weighed down to scoop creatures from the sea floor, can badly damage the seabed and other sea life.

As we travel on, we see the landscape changing. We notice cliffs made of red sandstone and white chalk, and long sandy beaches filled with holiday-makers. Children are paddling, windsurfers are trying new tricks and small sailing boats are catching the breeze. Some tall chalk features have characterful names such as Old Harry, Old Harry's Wife and the Needles. Near the Needles the English ships fired their cannons at the Spanish Armada, to prevent it from sailing between the Isle of Wight and mainland England. This protected two great ports of southern England: Southampton and Portsmouth. What tales these cities could tell, of Henry V's soldiers setting off for victory in the battle of Agincourt in 1415, of Henry VIII's favourite warship the *Mary Rose* sinking in 1545 and being raised from the sea hundreds of years later, of the Pilgrim Fathers setting out for the New World in 1620, and the D-Day

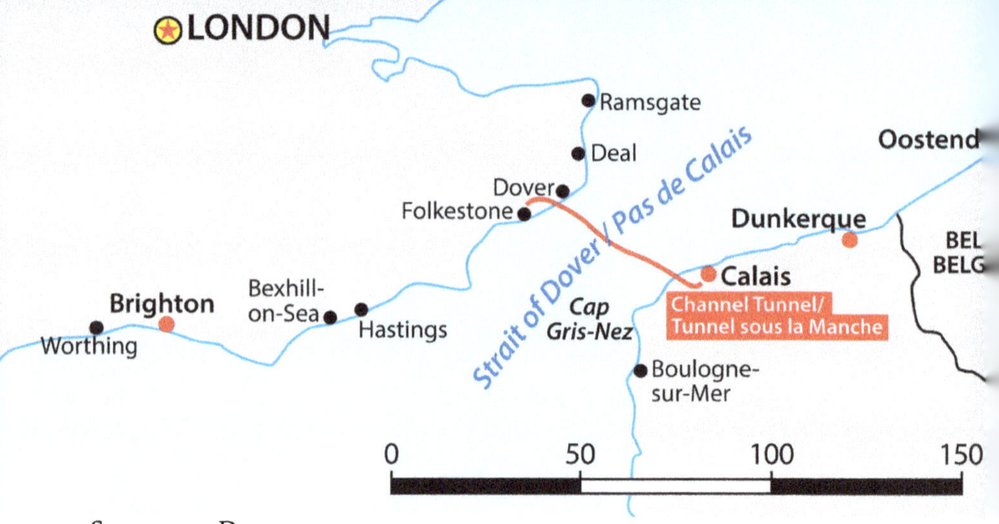

mission in 1944, which turned the tide of the Second World War.

Further on, much of the south-east coast of England is lined with pebble beaches, like the one near Hastings where William the Conqueror arrived with his army from Normandy in 1066. There are also chalk cliffs such as the famous White Cliffs of Dover where a magnificent clifftop castle overlooks the busy harbour and, just 20 miles away, the coast of France.

This narrowest part of the English Channel is called the Strait of Dover, and it can be crossed by ferry in 90 minutes or by an underground train in 35 minutes, through a tunnel which goes right under the sea, and comes up on the other side

at the French town of Calais. It can even be swum in 10 hours, though swimmers must plan very carefully because the Dover Strait is the busiest shipping lane in the world, with around 500 ships travelling through it every day.

The Spanish Armada waited near Calais, hoping to collect an army to invade England. The English navy thwarted their plans by sending eight blazing fire ships in amongst them. Terrified Spanish sailors cut their anchor ropes, and the scattered ships fled into the North Sea.

Let us follow their route and travel northwards past the mudflats of the wide estuary of the River Thames. Here at Tilbury, just east of London, Queen Elizabeth I rallied her troops, dressed in armour. If you go to Tilbury now, you can see an invasion of a different kind: a huge port is full of ships unloading their cargoes of food, machinery, grain and timber. Tall cranes lift metal containers from the ships. The containers are stacked like building blocks onto trucks and trains, and taken all around the country.

We sail on, around East Anglia, passing the creeks of Essex and the wide sandy beaches of Suffolk and Norfolk. The

HUNDREDS OF THOUSANDS OF WADING BIRDS VISIT THE WASH

waves and storms have done mighty work here, eroding the sand from one shore and depositing it at another. The Suffolk town of Dunwich has been lost to the sea, while the Norfolk town of Kings Lynn, which was once next to the coast, now stands three miles inland. The power of nature is turned into electricity by hundreds of white wind turbines, which we can see standing tall above the waves, out to sea. Further round the Norfolk coast is a large shallow bay called The Wash, where several rivers meet as they reach the sea. It has salt marshes, shingle and even quicksand—be careful!— and in the winter it is visited by hundreds of thousands of wading birds who feast in its lagoons. Don't forget to look out for colonies of seals and for King John's crown jewels! It is thought that the unpopular king lost them here in 1216 when his carts tried to cross the bay and got caught by the rising tide.

Sailing north, we pass the flat, sandy Lincolnshire coast,

Bamburgh Castle, Northumberland

the Humber estuary and the cliffs of North Yorkshire. Cover your ears as we go past Flamborough Head! Half a million seabirds are calling from their nests in the nooks and crannies in the chalk cliffs. At Whitby we notice a ruined abbey on the clifftop, and a staircase of 199 steps down to the town where Captain James Cook learnt to master a ship. In the harbour today there is a replica of his ship, the *Endeavour*, on which he discovered New Zealand and Australia. Beyond the cliffs of rural North Yorkshire, we sail past the tall chimneys of factories around Middlesbrough, and the beautiful beaches and dramatic castles of Northumberland, all the way to Scotland.

Dover Castle,
strategically located at
the Strait of Dover, is
described as the "Key to England"

chapter 6

The Coast of the British Isles

WE CONTINUE TO follow the route of the Spanish Armada as we trace the coast of Scotland. The east coast of Scotland has several large inlets, where major rivers meet the sea in wide v-shaped estuaries known locally as 'firths'. The first one that we come to is the Firth of Forth, where we find Scotland's capital city, Edinburgh. Just west of the city, the firth is still a mile wide and spanned by three impressive bridges. The most famous is the red cantilever rail bridge, which opened in 1890. The saying goes that as soon as workers have finished painting this long bridge, it's time to start again!

We pass the coast of Fife with its grassy chalk hills, fossil-rich limestone and quiet sand dunes, and notice the ruined castle and famous golf courses of St Andrews, called 'the home of golf'. The next large estuary, the Firth of Tay, is lined with sand, mud flats and reed beds. The reeds were once used by the local people to thatch the roofs of their houses; now they provide a home for many species of birds. The sandstone cliffs and wide sandy beaches of the Tayside coast give way to the

rugged cliffs of the Grampian east coast. As we reach the harbour city of Aberdeen we must look out for the many dolphins in these waters. Further up the coast Peterhead and St Fergus are busy fishing towns that also work hard to provide energy to the country. Peterhead is an important port for those who work in the North Sea's oil fields, and St Fergus' gas terminal processes and distributes a quarter of the UK's natural gas. The coastline turns a sharp corner west at Fraserburgh, where we can see Scotland's oldest lighthouse and many fishing boats laden with fresh shellfish.

Perhaps the captains of the Spanish Armada thought that all of Scotland had the kind of calm shingle beaches and sand dunes they had seen on the east coast, and that they would have smooth sailing all the way back to Spain.

Unfortunately for them the northern and western coast of Scotland is much more rugged and rocky. If you look at a map you will see the many grooves that cut deep into the western coast of Scotland. These are steep, deep sea lochs which were carved by glaciers and then flooded with water when sea levels rose thousands of years ago. Here, high winds and Atlantic waves batter the coast, especially in the storms of the autumn and winter months and it's not surprising that the north-west point of Scotland is called Cape Wrath. And at a place called Corryvreckan the tidal currents swirl to create a huge whirl-pool, one of the biggest in the world. Stormy weather forced the Spanish ships dangerously close to cliffs and sharp rocks. Further south, they followed the west coast of Ireland, which is now called the Wild Atlantic Way, for a good reason! The windswept coastline and towering cliffs offered them no shelter, and many ships were dashed against the rocks or sank in the raging waters. Indeed, half of the ships and three quarters of the men never made it back to Spain.

This historic defeat of the Spanish went a long way to establishing England as the most powerful maritime nation in the world. This power endured until the early twentieth century, and for hundreds of years, English, and later British, ships sailed rivers, seas and oceans, navigating, exploring, trading, settling and battling other lands all around the world.

The legacy of this maritime power can be seen as we finish our tour, by viewing some important port cities on the west

CAPE WRATH FROM THE SEA   CORRYVRECKAN WHIRLPOOL

coast of Britain and the east coast of Ireland. Bristol and Liverpool, Glasgow, Dublin and Belfast thrived on the opportunities to build ships and trade overseas, throughout the British Empire and beyond. Sadly, many ports were also involved in the transatlantic slave trade. During the eighteenth century, ships carried cloth and pottery from the British Isles to west Africa, then they transported enslaved African people across the Atlantic Ocean to the Caribbean, and finally brought sugar and cotton back to Britain. The terrible slave trade ended in the British Empire in 1807, through the efforts of campaigners such as William Wilberforce, though as recently as 2020 a crowd in Bristol pulled down a statue of a slave-trader and threw it into the harbour.

From the Bristol Channel round to Liverpool's Mersey estuary, we travel through the Irish Sea, between the beautiful coasts of Wales and Ireland. The south coast of Wales has some

WILD ATLANTIC WAY OFF THE WEST COAST OF IRELAND

A Cruise Liner at Liverpool's Cruise Terminal

important ports, and the north has several majestic castles. While over in Ireland, Dublin Bay looks as inviting now as it did to the Viking invaders of the ninth century. For the most part, however, all we can see is unspoilt countryside with sandy coves sheltered by dramatic cliffs. Dolphins swim beside our boat, puffins flap past and gannets dive gracefully into the sea. As we approach Liverpool, we glimpse in the distance the vast sandy shore of Blackpool beach, and the wide Morecambe Bay beyond.

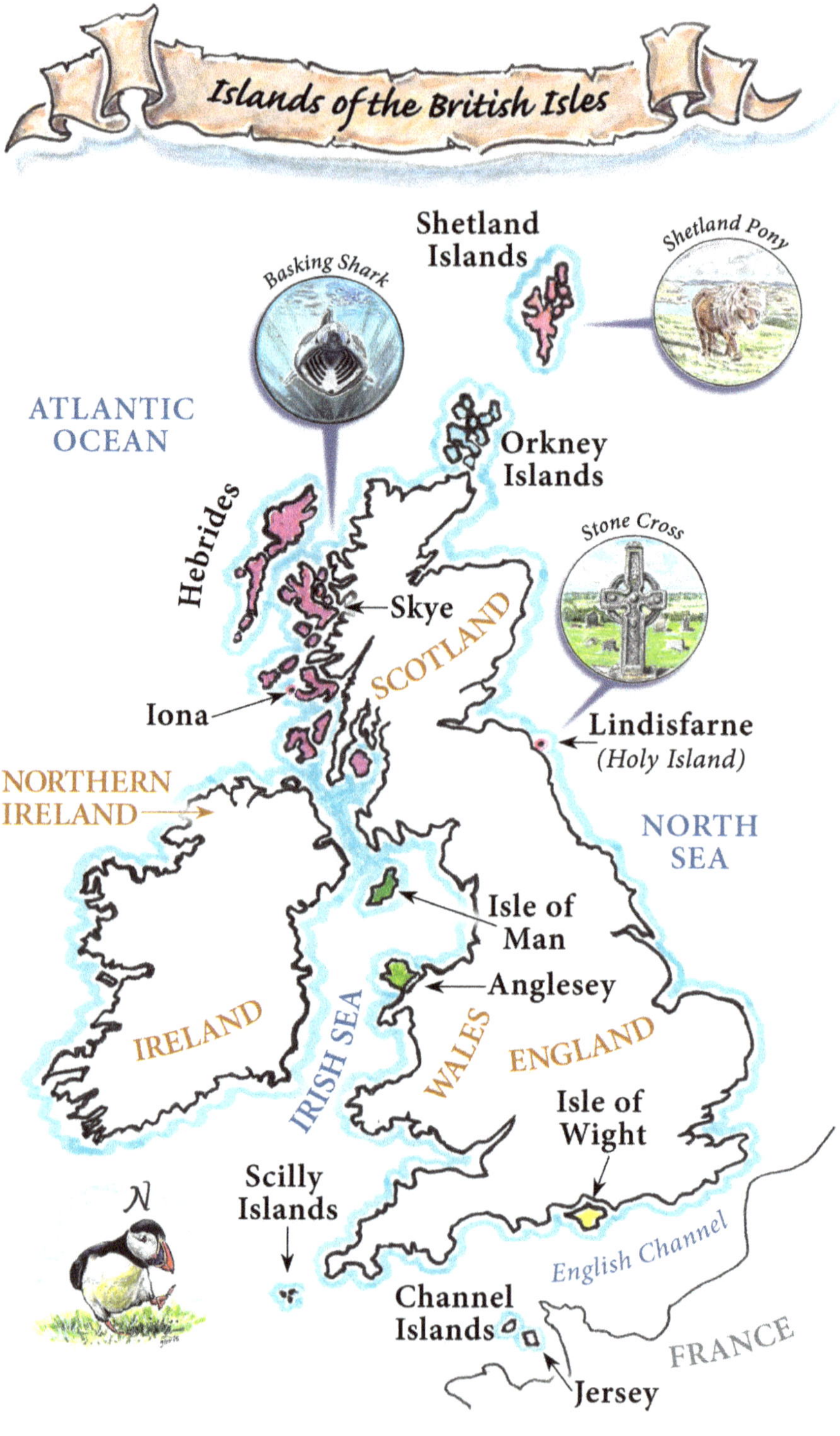

Islands of the British Isles

Basking Shark
Shetland Islands
Shetland Pony
ATLANTIC OCEAN
Orkney Islands
Stone Cross
Hebrides
Skye
SCOTLAND
Iona
Lindisfarne
(Holy Island)
NORTHERN IRELAND
NORTH SEA
Isle of Man
Anglesey
IRELAND
IRISH SEA
WALES
ENGLAND
Isle of Wight
N
Scilly Islands
English Channel
Channel Islands
FRANCE
Jersey

chapter 7

The Islands of the British Isles

WE HAVE ALREADY been introduced to the two largest islands of the British Isles: Great Britain and Ireland. But did you know, there are more than six thousand smaller islands in the seas surrounding Britain and Ireland? These also count as British Isles. Perhaps you can find some of them on a map. Some islands are in groups, such as the Hebrides, Orkneys and Shetlands off the coast of Scotland and the Isles of Scilly, off the south-west tip of England. Some are relatively big and stand alone such as the Isle of Wight, off the south coast of England; Anglesey, off the coast of Wales; and then the Isle of Man, which sits right in the middle of the Irish Sea, between England, Scotland, Ireland and Wales.

There is a small group of islands in the English Channel, between England and France, which are known as the Channel Islands. The largest, called Jersey, is famous for beautiful pale brown Jersey cows, whose milk makes delicious cream and ice cream. The Channel Islands are remarkable because they are actually much closer to France than they are to Britain. Why then, are they part of the British Isles and not part of France? It all goes back to the time of William the Conqueror,

who was Duke of Normandy in northern France. William invaded England in 1066, and when he became King of England, Normandy and the Channel Islands became part of the English Crown's lands. Over many centuries of battles and sieges the kings of England lost Normandy to the kings of France, but the Channel Islands still belong to the English Crown. During the Second World War, the Channel Islands were the only part of the British Isles to be occupied by the German armed forces.

At the opposite end of the British Isles you can find the Hebrides, a wild and remote group of islands off the west coast of Scotland. Looking on your map, you will see that they are the most north-westerly part of the UK, and that there is nothing but the Atlantic Ocean between them and the coast of North America, over three thousand miles away. The islands contain

bold mountains and pristine white beaches, formed from the shells of millions of sea creatures. Local farmers, known as crofters, fertilise their land with seaweed from the beaches, and the meadows are a haven for wildlife. Forty thousand barnacle geese from Greenland arrive every autumn, having flown non-stop for two days and nights, to spend the winter grazing on the islands' green grass. Basking sharks glide mysteriously through the water, while fish eagles soar through the air. Many islanders can speak Gaelic, and there is a strong tradition of weaving tweed and distilling whisky.

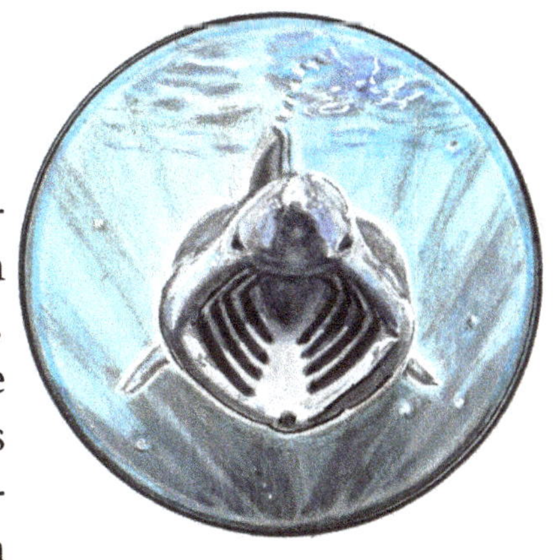

Some islands are known for their special spiritual heritage. In AD563 an Irish monk called Columba sailed from Ireland to Iona, an island in the Hebrides. St Columba and his followers founded a monastery on Iona which became a base for missionary journeys, spreading the Christian faith throughout Scotland and northern England. The islanders carved stone crosses and painted illuminated manuscripts, and it is thought that many Scottish Kings were buried on the island, including Shakespeare's famous Macbeth. In AD635, an Anglo-Saxon

Islands of the Outer Hebrides

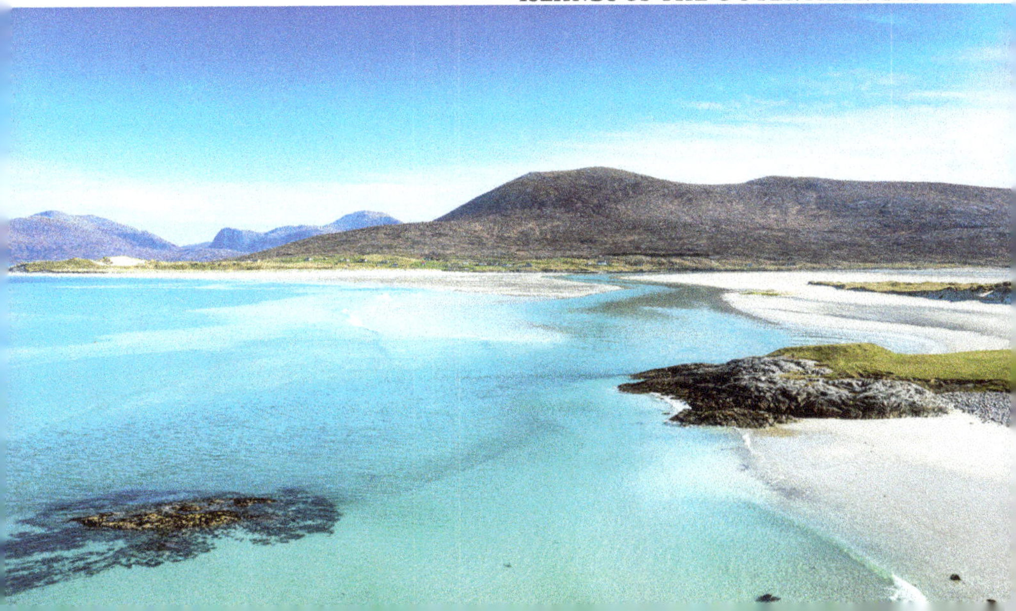

king called Oswald ruled Northumbria, which is now north-east England. King Oswald asked a monk called Aidan to come from Iona and start a monastery in his kingdom. The place he chose was a tiny island called Lindisfarne. Lindisfarne is connected to the mainland by a long road, or causeway, but twice a day, at high tide, it becomes an island. Indeed, for hundreds of years Lindisfarne has been known as Holy Island. St Aidan's monastery became a centre for learning, and was home to another saint, Cuthbert. The monks created a richly decorated manuscript of part of the Bible, known as the Lindisfarne Gospels, which is considered a masterpiece of

HOLY ISLAND, LINDISFARNE OFF THE NORTHUMBRIAN COAST

Anglo-Saxon art. Sadly, both Lindisfarne and Iona suffered attacks by the marauding Vikings; and later their Benedictine monasteries were closed during the Protestant Reformation in the sixteenth century. Now, though, several of the buildings have been restored and once again many pilgrims visit these islands.

Cities of the British Isles

N
NORTH
SEA
Glasgow
M8
Edinburgh
M74
Newcastle-
upon-Tyne
Londonderry
M2
Manchester
Belfast
M6
Leeds
M1
Blackpool
York
Dublin
Liverpool
Sheffield
M7
M6
M1
Limerick
Leicester
M8
Birmingham
Cambridge
Cork
Oxford
M11
M5
London
Cardiff
M4
Bristol
M3
M2
Dover
Bath
Southampton
Exeter
Plymouth
ATLANTIC
OCEAN

The Cities of the British Isles

THERE ARE MANY cities in the British Isles. London is by far the largest, and we will find out more about it in the next chapter. Let us look first at some of the other important cities and find out why cities came to exist at all. Close your eyes and imagine a city. Thousands and thousands of people live there, in street after street of houses and flats. In the centre there are shops and offices, museums and theatres, a cathedral and other places of worship; elsewhere there are schools and colleges, parks, sports grounds and swimming pools, a hospital and a university. People get around by bus or train, car or bike, and there are people just about everywhere. On the outskirts of the city there is even an airport and perhaps a zoo or a theme park. But did you know, cities like this are relatively new in the British Isles, and indeed in much of the world.

Close your eyes again and imagine going back in time. For many thousands of years, the people of the British Isles lived mostly in villages or very small towns and were busy farming the land, growing food to eat. Clothes and tools were made by hand in people's cottages or workshops, which took a long time. But in the eighteenth and nineteenth centuries, British inventors created coal-powered steam engines and made many other discoveries and inventions. These machines were soon used in vast factories or mills, where cloth could be woven and dyed and iron could be smelted much more quickly. This huge change-around in how things were made was called the Industrial Revolution. Thousands of people moved from the countryside to work in the factories, and rows and rows of houses were built for people to live in. Many cities grew up, particularly across the midlands and north of England, near coal mines and fast-flowing rivers. Perhaps you can find Birmingham, Leeds, Manchester and Sheffield on your map. These cities were all transformed by the growth of factories and textile mills. Port cities, such as Liverpool, Glasgow, Cardiff and Belfast became important places for building ships and trading with the rest of the world.

For many years Britain was the most industrialised land in the world and its cities were dark with the smoke and grime of hundreds of factories. Even today, many of the houses that you see in its cities were built during the eighteenth and nineteenth centuries, to house all the factory workers and their families. These workers often had a miserable experience, working long days in dangerous conditions. Instead of going to school, many children had to work up chimneys or down mines, and there were plenty of real-life Oliver Twists begging on the streets. Although it was hard for the poorest people, it was the Industrial Revolution that made Britain rich and powerful and so built up an Empire. This meant it controlled large parts of the world in Africa and Asia. When the Empire ended, some of its people came to live in Britain, in what is called immigration.

In the last hundred years or so, the cities have changed a great deal. Coal mines and factories have closed, because it is now cheaper for other countries to make many things. Some old factory buildings have been turned into flats, museums and art galleries. New kinds of factories have opened, which make food and medicines, cars and electric tools. Many cities are now full of people working in all kinds of different jobs: in science and art, developing computer software and running local government, in schools, hospitals, shops and offices. Unfortunately, many cities also have problems of pollution and unemployment, poverty and crime. By the middle of the twentieth century, many people were concerned that cities were growing too quickly and spoiling the countryside, so planners decided many cities should have a 'green belt'. This is a great green ring of countryside around a city, where laws prevent people from building houses. This protects a lot of farmland and woodland.

In some ways cities are alike, but there are also differences between different cities. Oxford and Cambridge have been

shaped by their famous universities. Brighton and Blackpool are popular with people enjoying a trip to the seaside. York, Bath and Chester are small cities with beautiful historic buildings, whereas Nottingham, Newcastle and Liverpool have large, modern city centres full of shops and businesses. Whatever their differences, all cities need to be linked to each other, especially by motorways, which enable people and goods to move around and get to the main centres for business and pleasure. There are also many people living in British cities whose families originally come from countries all over the world. You might meet Pakistanis in Bradford and Bangladeshis in Birmingham, and you might see the colourful carnivals in Leeds and Leicester, hosted by African-Caribbean communities.

In addition, each nation of the British Isles has a capital city, which has a special significance for the government, culture and economy of its own people. London is the capital of England and the UK as a whole; Edinburgh is the capital of Scotland; Cardiff is the capital of Wales; Belfast is the capital of Northern Ireland and Dublin is the capital of the Republic of Ireland. Each capital houses the national assembly or parliament, where elected politicians debate and make laws for the country. Capital cities are also home to national banks, businesses, charities and universities. Many people visit them as tourists and enjoy going to their theatres and museums. We will find out more about some cities and the kind of people who live there as we continue our tour around the British Isles, starting with London.

The British Museum
St. Paul's Cathedral
The Gherkin
N
Nelson's Column
Hyde Park
Globe Theatre
Tower of London
RIVER THAMES
The Royal Observatory, Greenwich
The London Eye
Big Ben/ Houses of Parliament
The Shard
Buckingham Palace
LONDON
gloris smith young ©

chapter 9

London

LET US DISCOVER London, the largest city in the British Isles and the capital city of England and the United Kingdom. We could travel around it in a 'black cab', as London taxis are known, or we could ride on a red double-decker London bus. We could even travel on the underground railway, called the 'tube'. But perhaps the best way to see the famous sights of this important city is to take a walk. Let us start on the north bank of the river Thames, on the site where the ancient Romans built a town. They called it Londinium, and it had protective walls, a fort and an amphitheatre. The Romans chose a good location, as the tidal river Thames was an easy way to connect with the sea and the rest of the Roman Empire. After the Romans left, the Anglo-Saxons lived here, and when the Normans arrived they made it the capital of England. Parts of the Roman and Medieval walls survive to this day. Today this area, just a square mile, is the City of London, the main financial district. The Bank of England is here with all its gold in deep vaults behind thick high walls.

When William the Conqueror invaded England in 1066, he built a tower by the river to guard the city of London. This

white tower is now the central keep of the Tower of London, a royal palace. Over the centuries it has housed the crown jewels, exotic animals and many famous prisoners, who often arrived by boat through the Traitor's Gate. Even Queen Elizabeth I was imprisoned here when she was a princess, but, unlike many, she survived to tell the tale. Not far away, in 1666, the Great Fire of London started at the king's baker's shop in Pudding Lane. It swept through the city, burning houses and churches, including St Paul's Cathedral. A tall column was built by Sir Christopher Wren as a monument to the great fire, and if we climb the spiral staircase inside the monument, we get a fantastic view across the historic square mile.

First, there is the beautiful dome of the new St Paul's Cathedral, also built by Wren, where there are monuments to British heroes such as the Duke of Wellington. Next to the Tower of London we see the tall, elegant Tower Bridge crossing the river. Meanwhile all around we see soaring skyscrapers of the many banks which thrive in this part of the city. Some modern buildings have surprising shapes and funny names, such as the Shard, the Gherkin and the Walkie-Talkie.

Let us continue to walk beside the river, along the Victoria Embankment. This tree-lined path was built in the nineteenth century to replace the marshy riverbanks. On the far side of the Thames we can see the Globe, a wonderful reconstruction of an Elizabethan theatre. Here a crowd stands in the open-air to watch Shakespeare's plays as they would have done hundreds of years ago. We then come to Trafalgar Square and marvel at Nelson's column, which towers high above the square in honour of the great naval hero who fought Napoleon. His statue is surrounded by magnificent lions and fountains on which children love to clamber. A magnificent building dominates the Square. It has a dome and columns and many steps leading up to it. Is it a palace or a temple? No, this is the National Gallery of Art, with the National Portrait Gallery behind it, and they are both filled with masterpieces from across the ages. This part of London, known as the West End, is famous for

SOME OF THE MODERN BUILDINGS IN THE LONDON SKYLINE

its many museums and theatres, shops and restaurants. If we want to see the grand parks and palaces of London, we must keep walking, and follow the river as it bends southwards, to Westminster.

Westminster Abbey was originally built by the Anglo-Saxon king Edward the Confessor in 1065, and ever since then it has been a place where kings and queens are crowned, married and buried. Next to the abbey is the parliament building, the Palace of Westminster with its famous clock tower, which contains the bell known as Big Ben. The Prime Minister's house, 10 Downing Street, is close by, along with all the offices of the government. In these buildings the politicians and civil servants meet, debate, vote and determine the laws of the land. Across the river is a great big ferris wheel called the London Eye. Just a short walk away is the beautiful royal residence of Buckingham Palace, which is guarded by soldiers wearing bright red uniforms and tall, black, bearskin hats. We are weary now from all our walking. Just imagine if we were invited into the palace for a snack! We don't have time today to look round all the museums. It would take days and days to see all the dinosaur skeletons, Egyptian mummies, tanks and teddy bears. We will have to come back another time!

Even though we have seen so many things, this is really

PALACE OF WESTMINSTER AND BIG BEN

just the very centre of London. London is such an important and busy city that it has grown and grown over hundreds of years and Greater London is like many towns that have all joined together. More than nine million people live here, which is far too many to talk to, but let us imagine a couple of families. Theo lives in Enfield in North London. He walks to school with his friends who, like him, love playing cricket, and you can see the Enfield Cricket Club from the end of his road. On their way home they sometimes buy sweets at the Caribbean food shop where Theo's aunt works. Theo's great-grandparents moved to London from Jamaica, but everyone else in his family has lived in London all their lives. His big brother Darren travels on the tube every day to work in one of the West End theatres and his sister Jade works in a bank in the City. Theo's friend Ansh and his family moved here from India when he was a baby. His sister Chaitra hopes to be a doctor like their dad when she grows up, and work in one of the many London hospitals, but Ansh would prefer to drive an underground train. If they end up travelling into central London for work, they will join more than a million other people who make that journey every day, many by train to stations like Kings Cross or Paddington.

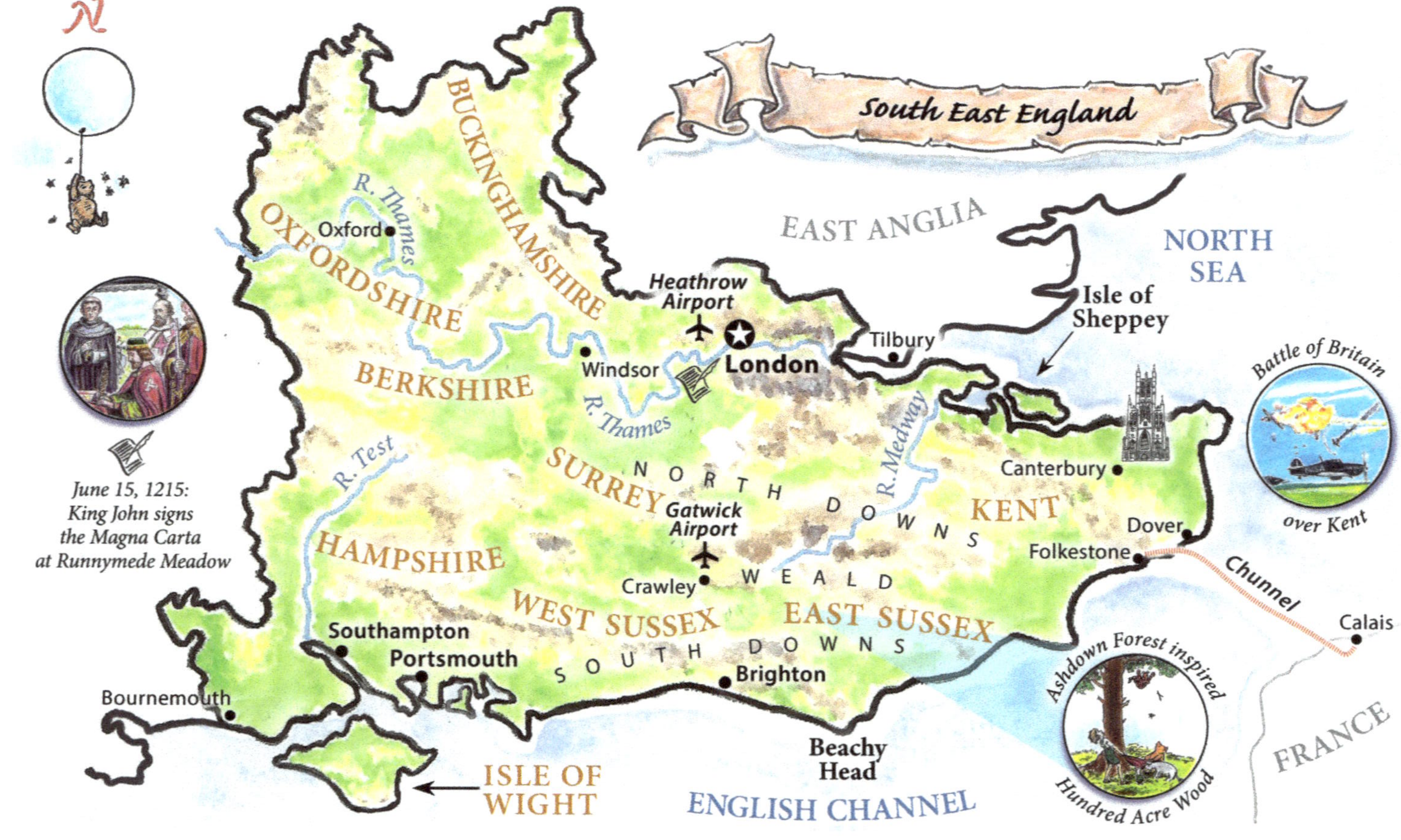

N
South East England
EAST ANGLIA
NORTH SEA
OXFORDSHIRE
Oxford
R. Thames
BUCKINGHAMSHIRE
Heathrow Airport
Windsor
London
Tilbury
Isle of Sheppey
BERKSHIRE
R. Thames
June 15, 1215:
King John signs
the Magna Carta
at Runnymede Meadow
R. Test
HAMPSHIRE
SURREY
Gatwick Airport
Crawley
NORTH DOWNS
R. Medway
Canterbury
KENT
Dover
Folkestone
Battle of Britain over Kent
WEALD
WEST SUSSEX
EAST SUSSEX
Chunnel
Calais
Southampton
Portsmouth
SOUTH DOWNS
Brighton
Ashdown Forest inspired
Hundred Acre Wood
FRANCE
Bournemouth
Beachy Head
ISLE OF WIGHT
ENGLISH CHANNEL

chapter 10

South East England

LET US CONTINUE our tour of the British Isles. We have started in London, which is in the south-eastern corner of England, and the area around London is often known as the Home Counties. Counties, sometimes called Shires, are smaller parts of a country, looked after by a local government, and they usually contain many towns and villages. The Home Counties are often thought of as leafy and green, with traditional villages, cricket pitches and tea shops. By the middle of the twentieth century, though, many people were concerned about how big and overcrowded London had become, and thought it might keep spreading and spreading. So London, like many British cities, was given a 'green belt'. At the same time, several new towns were designed and built in the Home Counties, so that people could live there instead. If you could design a new town, what would it be like? What would the houses look like? Would it have a cinema and a fish and chip shop? How would people get around? Maybe it would have lots of cycle paths or an underground railway?

One of the new towns built near London is called Crawley. Let's imagine a boy called Henry who lives there. He likes it because it has lots of wooded parks and lakes for everyone to share. It's only a short train ride to get into London, where his mum works, while his dad works just up the road in the head office of a big supermarket. Many of the people who work in London actually have their homes in the Home Counties surrounding London, and they travel in and out—commuting—every day by car or train. Henry and his parents also travel into London quite often to enjoy visiting the shops and museums, and to fly away on holiday from one of London's airports like Gatwick or Heathrow. Railways and motorways head in and out of London in every direction, like a giant cobweb, connecting with the cities, towns and villages in other parts of the country.

Further from the capital, the countryside in this part of England is characterised by gentle rolling hills and vales. The chalk hills, known as the North and South Downs, form white

CRAWLEY NEW TOWN

ROLLING HILLS OF THE NORTH DOWNS

cliffs where they meet the sea, such as at Beachy Head in East Sussex, and the famous White Cliffs of Dover in Kent. This fertile farming country is suitable for many types of crops, such as barley, wheat, corn, hops and potatoes. Meanwhile sheep clamber on the scarp slopes and cows graze on the grassy clay valleys. Kent has traditionally been known as the Garden of England, because fruit such as apples and cherries thrive in its warm, dry climate. At the heart of Kent is Canterbury, a small city with a beautiful cathedral, first built following the visit of St Augustine in AD 597, who brought Christianity to the south of England. During the Second World War the skies above Kent were full of British planes—Spitfires and Hurricanes—desperately fighting back the waves of German bombers in what was called the Battle of Britain. Their victory saved Britain from a Nazi invasion.

On the coast there are several great ports and seaside towns. Dover's ferries carry people to and from France, Southampton is crowded with huge liners and oil tankers that travel

the world and Portsmouth is an important naval base. Near Folkestone there is the Channel Tunnel which travels over 31 miles under the sea bed to France carrying the superfast Eurostar trains. Bournemouth is a large seaside town which has seven miles of sandy beaches. Further inland, there is lots of unspoilt countryside, such as the New Forest, which William the Conqueror established as a royal hunting ground, and the Ashdown Forest, the setting for A. A. Milne's Winnie the Pooh stories. Children enjoy camping, picnicking and horse-riding in these parks and forests during their holidays.

The other path we must trace while we are here is the valley of the important river Thames. We have already heard that it follows a leisurely, easterly course from the Cotswold hills in Gloucestershire, to London and the North Sea. But climb with me into a boat near its source, and let us imagine what we would see along the way. The narrow river meanders slowly through gentle vales, and the first city it reaches is Oxford. Oxford is called the 'city of dreaming spires' because of the many historic church steeples and college chapels. There are also renowned research hospitals, publishing houses and car factories, which produce over a thousand MINIs every day! On the river here we see students and tourists gliding on wide, flat-bottomed boats called punts, trying to avoid falling in the water! We pass White Horse Vale, named after the giant outline of a horse, which was cut into the chalky hilltop in prehistoric times, and we enjoy the quiet beech woods which cover the valley slopes. Next we come to the patch of river that inspired Kenneth Grahame's tales of the Wind in the Willows, and we can almost imagine Mr Toad and his friends here, enjoying 'messing about in boats'. Soon the magnificent towers of Windsor Castle loom high on the horizon, and we pass the meadows of Runnymede where King John signed the Magna Carta in 1215. The Magna Carta insisted that everyone, including kings, must obey the law, and has inspired people all over the world to campaign for justice and freedom. We climb out of our boat on the outskirts of London to explore Hampton Court Palace. In its Tudor great hall we meet actors dressed as Henry VIII and one of his six unfortunate wives. We imagine the music and feasting with which Cardinal Wolsey entertained the king and his court, and see the spits turning in the magnificent kitchen fireplaces. Outside, we can smell the sweet scent of the enormous rose garden and enjoy getting lost in the maze.

HAMPTON COURT ON THE RIVER THAMES

South West England
WALES
Marlborough Downs
Bristol
Bath
BRISTOL CHANNEL
R. Avon
Mendips
Cherhill Chalk Horse
N
Exmoor
Somerset Levels
SOMERSET
WILTSHIRE
R. Parrett
DEVON
DORSET
Gallos~Ghost King Statue at Tintagel Castle
R. Exe
Exeter
Poole
Stonehenge
Bodmin Moor
R. Tamar
Dartmoor
Plymouth
CORNWALL
ENGLISH CHANNEL
Land's End

chapter 11

South West England

Look again at the map of England, and find the south-west corner. The counties of the South West are Cornwall and Devon, Dorset, Somerset and Wiltshire. We start exploring at the furthest tip of Cornwall, at the point called Land's End. It is rocky and wild, surrounded by crashing waves and granite cliffs which jut out into the restless sea. As you can see, this corner of England is a peninsula, meaning that it is surrounded by water on three sides. Indeed, Cornwall is almost entirely cut off from the rest of the country by the river Tamar which runs along the border with its neighbour, Devon. Such a remote corner of the country made an excellent stronghold for the Celts. Celtic people, called Britons, lived in the British Isles before and during the time of the Roman Empire. Later, Celtic Britons in Cornwall held out against the Anglo-Saxon invaders for hundreds of years, and Cornish, a Celtic language, was spoken by some until the nineteenth century. Even today the Cornish people are recognised as a minority group who have a distinctive identity.

We stand on a granite cliff top, and look out over the rough sea. Below us are craggy rocks and rock pools, and further up the coast there is a sheltered cove with a fine sandy beach. Inland we explore the bleak peaks of Bodmin Moor, which is scattered with ancient standing stones. As we scramble over boulders and heather, we meet a local family walking their dog. The little girl has a traditional Cornish name, Demelza. In the distance we see a tall brick chimney. Demelza tells us that the chimney is all that is left of the engine house of an old tin mine. The land under our feet is rich in minerals, especially tin and copper ores, that were mined here for thousands of years. Demelza's grandad used to work in a tin mine, taking a cornish pasty with him for his lunch. Most mines are closed now. Instead, a lot of the local people work in jobs that look after the many tourists that visit every summer, to enjoy the beautiful countryside and sandy beaches. Demelza's dad rents out holiday cottages, and her mum works in a café near the sea. Their local speciality is cream tea, a pot of tea with fresh scones, strawberry jam and clotted cream. Demelza enjoys eating the scones almost as much as finding out about

STOWES HILL ON BODMIN MOOR

local legends. She tells us about a ruined castle by the sea, at a place called Tintagel. Legend has it that King Arthur was born there, and that his sword, Excalibur, was thrown into a lake up here on Bodmin Moor. Perhaps it is still there, hidden beneath the waters.

It's time for us to continue our tour of South West England by crossing the River Tamar into Devon. We notice the great peaks, or 'tors', of Dartmoor and Exmoor, and the ponies that roam freely over the moors. We see the ancient city of Exeter and its beautiful Norman cathedral adorned with dozens of carved figures from the Bible. We enter Dorset which, like Devon, is mostly given to grassy pasture or farmed for barley, potatoes, flowers and fruit. These thrive in the South West's warm climate, which is the mildest in the UK. Cows are reared for their beef and milk, and some of the milk becomes delicious clotted cream. The sea-side is very popular with tourists, and children in this part of the country enjoy paddling and swimming in the shallow sea. The more adventurous try surfing in the breaking waves and hunt for spiky sea urchins in rock pools. Some places, such as the Jurassic Coast of Dorset are excellent for finding fossils, while the harbour walls of small fishing towns are often full of children 'crabbing'. 'Crabbing' means catching crabs by dangling a fishing line with a bit of bacon or fish as bait.

Dorset, Somerset and Wiltshire formed the western part of the Anglo-Saxon kingdom of Wessex – the West Saxons. Beautiful ridges of hills surround a large flat area known as the Somerset Levels, which is barely above sea level. Somerset, 'the land of the summer people' was too wet and marshy to live in for much of the year, and King Alfred the Great was able to hide here when his kingdom of Wessex was threatened by Viking invaders. Now, the land is protected from flooding by man-made banks and pumps, and cows graze among the willows, which are used for basket-weaving. The most remarkable features of Wiltshire, up on its chalk downs—where a down is an up—are the ancient sites of Stonehenge and Avebury. These circles of giant stones, great ditches and barrows are masterpieces of prehistoric engineering, but quite how and why they were built remains a mystery.

The twin cities of Bristol and Bath must not be neglected. The Romans built a town at Bath to enjoy bathing in the hot springs which naturally emerge there. It was just as popular with the rich people of the eighteenth-century, who rebuilt it into an elegant little city, full of beautiful Georgian houses and ballrooms, which

we see there today. Just thirteen miles away is Bristol, a bigger, bustling city with a history of trade and manufacturing. It is an excellent place to celebrate the Victorian engineer, Isambard Kingdom Brunel. His Clifton Suspension Bridge, begun in 1831, had the longest span of any bridge in the world at that time, and it still stands majestically above a gorge over the River Avon. In the harbour we can see Brunel's great ship, the *SS Great Britain*, one of the first made of iron and with a propeller. We can enjoy travelling on Brunel's Great Western Railway, which links the South West to the rest of the country.

The West Midlands

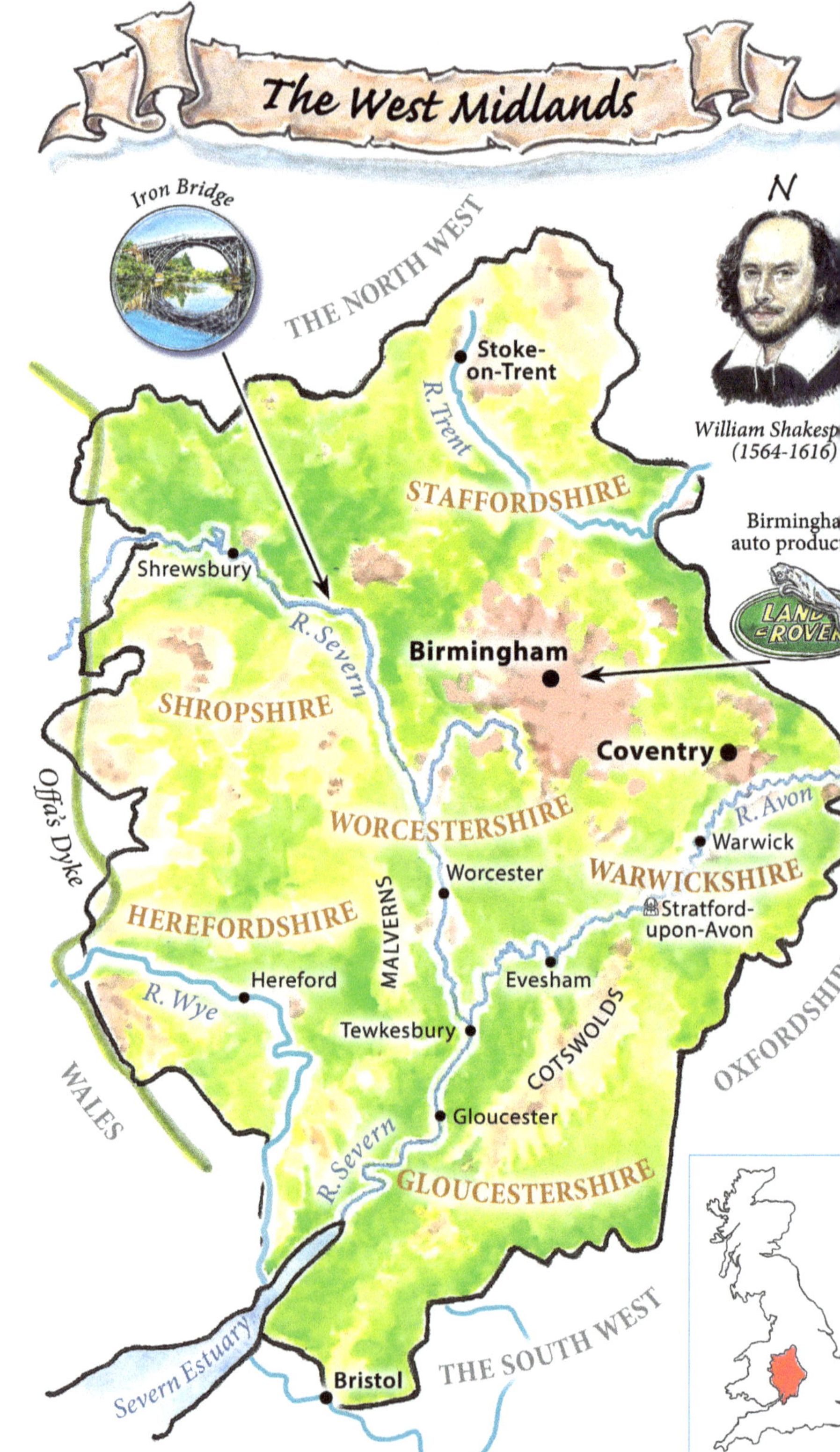

chapter 12

The West Midlands

THE WEST MIDLANDS, more than most regions, is a tale of two sides. Two very different landscapes and histories characterise the region, the rural and the urban, lush green countryside and busy, industrial towns. Let us begin with the rural. The beautiful Cotswold hills begin with a steep escarpment above the Avon and Severn rivers in the west and their rolling hills extend through Gloucestershire, Oxfordshire and Warwickshire in central England. The picturesque Cotswold landscape has ancient beech woodlands and limestone grasslands. Nestled between the hills are pretty villages and market towns built from honey-coloured limestone. Many villages, like Chipping Camden, have large medieval 'wool churches'. These were not built out of wool, but using money from merchants who prospered by selling wool from the sheep that roamed the hills. To the north-west of the Cotswolds lies the fertile Vale of Evesham. This wide valley, centred around the town of Evesham and the winding River Avon, is full of orchards and vegetable gardens, growing plums, brussels sprouts, asparagus and peas. Choose your favourite and have a munch as we follow the Avon. We could go upstream and

discover the historic towns of Warwick and Stratford, where England's most famous writer, William Shakespeare, was born. But instead let us follow it downstream, to the town of Tewkesbury. Here it meets an even greater river, the glorious River Severn.

The Severn is Britain's longest river. It rises in the slopes of Plynlimon in Wales and, along with the rivers Trent and Wye, it keeps this hilly part of England lush and fertile. Shropshire, Staffordshire, Herefordshire and Worcestershire are all dominated by agriculture, and their green fields provide grazing and fodder for sheep and cows. We particularly notice the Hereford breed of cattle, with their red bodies and white faces. Amongst all this beautiful greenery, there are traces of the settlements and industrial activity of the past. A huge long earthen wall and ditch, called Offa's Dyke, and many Norman castles reveal that this was once frontier territory, the fiercely contested borderlands between England and Wales. Centuries later, it was here at Coalbrookdale that great progress was made in the Industrial Revolution. A Quaker called Abraham Darby was the first person to smelt iron using coke, a type of coal, and this led to a surge in production of iron throughout the region. Nearby, his grandson, Abraham Darby III, built the world's first iron bridge. The bridge crosses a gorge in the Severn valley, and it was so momentous that the town where it was built is now called Ironbridge.

This leads us to the second side of our tour of the West Midlands, the towns and cities. In north Staffordshire, the coal and clay in the soil was just what was needed for making earthenware and china, and the city of Stoke-on-Trent became the world's centre for making pottery. Even today, children can enjoy having a go at making or painting clay pots and cups in its museums. Further south is the region known as the Black Country. At one time there were so many factories

BIRMINGHAM CAR FACTORY

and furnaces here, producing so much smoke and grime, that the place was said to be 'black by day and red by night' and may have inspired JRR Tolkein's descriptions of Mordor in *The Lord of the Rings*. Queen Victoria was apparently so disgusted with the industrial landscape that she closed her carriage curtains as she drove past! Now the towns are much cleaner, but more built-up than ever. The dirty industry has been replaced by factories using electricity to produce locks and keys, nuts, bolts and glassware.

Nearby, the second largest city in Britain spreads out across the land: Birmingham. Centuries ago, Birmingham's factories produced buttons, guns and jewellery. Now it is better known

SPAGHETTI JUNCTION IN BIRMINGHAM

for cars, aeroplanes and chocolate. The city is large and busy, with a thousand and one different trades and many attractions for visitors, such as theatres, shops and museums. The cities of the West Midlands are well connected to one another and the rest of England. First a network of canals was created, to transport coal, iron and goods. Now the busiest routes are motorways, railways and airports. One vast motorway junction has so many roads joining together that it is called Spaghetti Junction! These cities are densely populated with people whose families come from all over the world. They work in the factories, shops and hospitals, and worship in churches, mosques, synagogues and gurdwaras.

The East Midlands
Peak District
Chatsworth House
Sherwood Forest
YORKSHIRE
NORTH SEA
PENNINES
Humber Estuary
WOLDS
Lincoln
DERBYSHIRE
NOTTINGHAMSHIRE
R. Trent
R. Witham
LINCOLNSHIRE
R. Derwent
Nottingham
The Wash
Derby
Melton Mowbray
Loughborough
LEICESTERSHIRE
RUTLAND
Bosworth
Leicester
R. Soar
R. Welland
WEST MIDLANDS
EAST ANGLIA
Naseby
NORTHAMPTONSHIRE
R. Nene
Northampton
Sulgrave Manor
(home to the
English ancestors of
George Washington)

chapter 13

The East Midlands

THE EAST MIDLANDS covers a wide variety of land, from the high hills of the Peak District, dipping down to the long and wide Trent valley, to the rolling chalk wolds of Lincolnshire, and finally the sandy shore of the North Sea. Much of it once belonged to the Anglo-Saxon kingdom of Mercia. Let us start by exploring the bleak landscape of the Dark Peak.

Derbyshire's Peak District is at the southern end of the Pennines, the range of hills which stretch like a backbone down the middle of northern England. The Dark Peak is named after the steep crags of exposed gritstone, the purple heather and the black peat bogs of this high plateau. Further south is the White Peak, formed from limestone, which has gentler slopes and valleys, covered in grasslands and ash woods. Families love to walk and cycle in the hills, and also to explore the treasures hidden below the ground. What treasure is this? Over the ages, water has found its way through cracks in the limestone hills, and has gradually eroded great underground caverns and grottoes. These treasure troves are adorned with gems, as well as stalactites and stalagmites—limestone structures that look like icicles. Over the centuries, human miners have also carved out tunnels in their search for lead and other precious metal ores. Now we can explore these hidden worlds, though many require guidance from experts, safety equipment and a willingness to scramble, squeeze and even swim! Other visitors to the Peak District prefer to wander around the great stately homes like Chatsworth or eat the local dessert, Bakewell tart.

We leave the hills behind and visit Nottinghamshire, whose sandy soil was once covered by the great Sherwood Forest. According to the tales, which were first told over six hundred years ago, it was here that Robin Hood and his merry men hid from the Sheriff of Nottingham, stealing from the rich and giving to the poor. Parts of the Sherwood Forest still exist, and walkers and cyclists can discover ancient oaks alongside newer pine trees. Further east lies the wide valley of the River Trent, which snakes its way in a 'J' shape from Stoke, in the west, to the Humber estuary to the north-east, draining much of the East Midlands as it goes. Many dairy herds live near its banks and their milk is turned into a popular kind of cheese called

TRAILS IN THE PEAK DISTRICT

Stilton. Stilton often has blue veins and is a speciality of this region, it is not made anywhere else in the world.

Further south, we find several important cities and industries clustered together. Derby, Nottingham, Leicester and Loughborough sit near coal fields and were pioneers of new technology during the Industrial Revolution. James Hargreaves, inventor of the spinning jenny, built a factory at Nottingham and Sir Richard Arkwright built the first water-powered mill for spinning cotton at Cromford near Derby. Today children visiting on school trips dress up in costume and learn what it would have been like to work in the mill. Modern factories are very different, but across the region many people are still employed in making clothes and shoes, steel and cars. The cities are well connected by railways and by one of the country's most important motorways, the M1, which goes all the way from London to Leeds in Yorkshire.

While we are here, we can visit Bosworth Common, where in 1485 King Richard III was defeated by Henry VII, which began the Tudor age. Richard's body was discovered in 2012 underneath a car park in Leicester, on the site of an old chapel. The identity of the skeleton was confirmed when DNA tests matched the living descendants of his Plantagenet family, and the medieval king was given a formal reburial in Leicester Cathedral. In recent decades Leicester has become home to people

Stilton Cheese

whose families come from many different parts of the world. So many diverse communities live here that no group has a majority, and all sorts of colourful clothes and tasty food are sold in the streets. Every year thousands of people gather for a huge Diwali celebration, one of the largest outside India, when the streets are filled with bright lights and fireworks light up the sky.

Moving further southwards, amongst the rolling hills of Northamptonshire, we pass the site of another battle, Naseby. Here, on a foggy day in 1645, another king, Charles I, was defeated. At the top of the hill we see a memorial whose plaque reads, "From near this site Oliver Cromwell led the Cavalry charge which decided the issue of the battle and ultimately that of the great Civil War." Cromwell was the Puritan general who took seriously the English tradition that rulers should respect the people's freedom. Within a few months of this battle, Charles had surrendered, and in 1649 he was executed for treason. Later, yet another famous statesman and revolutionary would come from this part of England. A Tudor house called Sulgrave Manor was home to the English ancestors of George Washington. George Washington led the fight against British rule in America and, in 1789, he became the first president of the United States. Now school children visit Sulgrave Manor house and orchard dressed in Tudor costume, to find out about Tudor life, games and toys.

A trip through the East Midlands would not be complete without a visit to the seaside, so let's follow the Fosse Way, the ancient Roman road, to Lincolnshire. We pass the small city of Lincoln with its great cathedral and travel over the chalk hills, called wolds. We see field after field of sugar beet, grains and vegetables, and finally, there it is, the North Sea. Lincolnshire's coast is long and sandy, dotted with small towns with beach huts and funfairs. On a fine day we could spend many hours here, enjoying paddling, donkey rides, sandcastles and fish and chips. While such days at the seaside are an enjoyable tradition, many British people also take holidays abroad, seeking warm summer weather near the Mediterranean, or going skiing in the Alps in the winter.

DONKEY RIDES AT THE SEASIDE

East Anglia
THE EAST MIDLANDS
NORTH SEA
Offshore Wind Farms
The Wash
N
R. Wensum
King's Lynn
Little Ouse
R. Nene
Great Ouse
NORFOLK
THE BROADS
Norwich
Peterborough
CAMBRIDGESHIRE
THE FENS
Ely
SUFFOLK
R. Waveney
Sutton Hoo
Great Ouse
Cambridge
R. Cam
Ipswich
Bedford
R. Orwell
Felixstowe
Harwich
HERTFORDSHIRE
R. Blackwater
Colchester
ESSEX
London
Tilbury
Thames Estuary
The Ports of
Felixstowe & Tilbury
THE SOUTH EAST

chapter 14

East Anglia

EAST ANGLIA is in the east of central England, north-east of London and sticking out into the North Sea like a big round dinner plate. It has some of the flattest, lowest land in Britain and its climate is also a bit dryer and warmer in the summer and a bit colder in the winter than the rest of the island. This is because the prevailing westerly winds that bring moisture from the Atlantic Ocean have usually dropped all their rain on other areas before they get here.

East Anglia was the name of the Anglo-Saxon kingdom which flourished here in the sixth to ninth centuries. The counties we now know as Norfolk and Suffolk were named after the 'north folk' and 'south folk' who lived here. The riches of the East Angles, were vividly revealed in the 1930s when Anglo-Saxon treasure was discovered at a burial mound in Sutton Hoo in Suffolk. Gold jewellery, silverware and an ornate helmet and sword had been buried inside the ship of a great warrior, or even a king. However, long before he lived and died, Norfolk was home to the Iceni, a warlike Celtic tribe who famously rebelled against the Romans in AD60. Led by their queen, Boudicca, the Iceni travelled south through the counties we now know as Suf-

folk and Essex and burned down London before they were finally defeated by Roman soldiers. Suffolk and Essex have gently rolling hills and would have been densely forested at that time. Now the land is farmed and scattered with pretty villages, and the coast is indented with tidal creeks. These pastoral landscapes inspired the artist John Constable, who loved painting church spires, fields and ponds. If you go there today you will find traditional timber-framed houses, painted pink or yellow and clustered around large 'wool churches', because this region, like the Cotswolds, was made rich in the Middle Ages by the flocks of sheep grazing on its slopes. There are several important ports, but it is huge metal containers, rather than sacks of wool, that are now shipped through Felixstowe and Tilbury; and every year a million passengers travel on ferries between Harwich and mainland Europe.

KING'S COLLEGE CHAPEL CAMBRIDGE

Further inland is the historic little city of Cambridge. Let's imagine a family who live there, Ella and Joshua and their parents. Their mum works at Cambridge University Press, which publishes educational books, and their dad is a scientist working in a laboratory to develop new medicines. Ella's dream is to study at Cambridge University, and she loves exploring the beautiful college buildings, and walking in the footsteps of Sir Isaac Newton, Charles Darwin and Sir David Attenborough. Joshua would rather be a farmer, and he loves seeing the cows grazing in the meadows close to the city centre.

For a holiday, the family sometimes goes sailing on the Broads east of Norwich. They are lakes joined by rivers which were originally medieval peat excavations which became flooded. Peat is partially decayed vegetation which was in the past an important source of fuel. But they also like to go on narrowboat trips on the nearby River Great Ouse. They love water. The Great Ouse is the fourth longest river in the UK, after the Severn, Thames and Trent, which we have already heard about. Ella is surprised to find that there are several River Ouses in the UK,

such as the Little Ouse, which joins the Great Ouse in Norfolk. But when she finds out that 'ouse' comes from the Celtic word that means 'water' she agrees that 'water' is a sensible name for a river! They hire the narrowboat at a town called Bedford, where they don't see any beds, but they do see the tall chimneys of an old brick factory. Wearing life jackets, they look out for swans and eels in the river and pass under old stone bridges at Huntingdon and St Ives. When they get to a lock, Joshua and Ella help to open the gates. The locks help manage the water level as the river goes down a slope. The children hardly notice the slope though, as they look out on a clear day, the large fields on the river banks look as flat as a tabletop, and they have long straight ditches running alongside them. Joshua is excited to see the tractors and combine harvesters in the golden fields, reaping the wheat and barley, which will be used for bread and animal fodder.

Their mum tells them that so much food is produced in this part of England that it is called the Breadbasket of Britain where the sunnier summers ripen the grain. It wasn't always like this though. Some parts of Norfolk and Cambridgeshire are so flat, and only just above sea level, that they are called fenland. Ella remembers that near Cambridge there are villages named after the fens, Fen Ditton and Fen Drayton. In years gone by, all the fenland was wet and marshy, and people survived by catching eels and ducks, and harvesting reeds and peat. The rare patches of higher ground such as the Isle of Ely were real islands, surrounded by water. Over the centuries, many people tried to drain the land, in ancient times the Romans built flood barriers, in the Middle Ages monks tried to clear the waterways and in the seventeenth century a Dutch engineer called Cornelius Vermuyden dug whole new rivers and drainage channels. As they travel along, their dad points out a huge sluice gate. This separates the Great Ouse from one of Vermuyden's 'new' rivers, although if there was a risk of flooding, the gate could be opened to take water directly towards the sea. Their boat trip ends at the cathedral city of Ely, which is no longer an island. Nearby the Great Ouse is joined by the River Cam from Cambridge, and they catch the train home. If they had gone further in their boat, they could have gone to Kings Lynn or linked up with the River Nene at Peterborough. Both the Nene and the Great Ouse would eventually have carried them out into the great marshy bay called the Wash. Peterborough, an important transport and commercial hub, has overtaken Norwich with its Norman castle and cathedral, and is now the largest city in East Anglia.

Yorkshire

White Rose of York
THE NORTH EAST
NORTH SEA
R. Tees
Middlesbrough
R. Swale
PENNINES
NORTH YORK MOORS
NORTH YORKSHIRE
YORKSHIRE DALES
Vale of York
R. Ouse
R. Foss
R. Derwent
YORKSHIRE WOLDS
R. Wharfe
York
THE NORTH WEST
EAST RIDING OF YORKSHIRE
Leeds
Bradford
R. Aire
R. Ouse
Hull
Huddersfield
WEST YORKSHIRE
R. Trent
Humber Bridge
Humber Estuary
SOUTH YORKSHIRE
Sheffield
R. Don
THE EAST MIDLANDS
N
W

chapter 15

Yorkshire

YORKSHIRE IS A huge and beautiful area of north-eastern England. It has a distinctive identity, the people here are proud to be Yorkshire folk and sometimes even call their land 'God's own country'! It has traditional food to be enjoyed, such as Wensleydale cheese and a gingerbread cake called parkin. Yorkshire pudding is a baked batter which goes very well with a roast dinner, one of British people's favourite meals. Yorkshire is now split into four counties, North Yorkshire, West Yorkshire, South Yorkshire and the East Riding of Yorkshire, and right in the middle, in the wide, flat Vale of York, is York itself.

Taking a walk through York is like walking through the whole history of England. On our walk we meet a boy called Tom, who offers to show us around. First, we see the tall, thick walls around the city centre. "These were first built by the Romans," Tom says. "Do you see where these two rivers meet? That's the River Foss and the River Ouse." (This is a different river Ouse from the ones in East Anglia, and we remember that Ouse comes from the Celtic word for 'water'.) "The Romans built a fortress here because two rivers meant

York was easy to defend, but also easy to get to from the North Sea. On the down side, it also means that it still floods pretty often and that lots of invaders came along! The Angles and then Vikings came from across the sea, up the river, took over the city and stayed here for hundreds of years. Even now lots of streets have Viking names, and every year there is a Viking festival where people dress up in costume, tell Viking stories and show you how to do crafts like weaving and leatherwork.'

Tom leads us up narrow, crooked streets built in the medieval times and past the towering cathedral, called York Minster. "It took more than 250 years to build the Minster, and it's the biggest gothic cathedral in England," Tom tells us. "York was the most important city in the north of England, and if you go out into the countryside, you'll see that Yorkshire has loads of ruined abbeys and castles. There were battles near here in the Wars of the Roses and the Civil War. Crowds of tourists come here from all over the world to see the old buildings. But my favourite thing about York are all the trains in the National Railway Museum and the chocolate from the chocolate factory!

SHAMBLES ALLEY IN YORK

When the wind blows in the right direction you can smell chocolate in the air! It makes me really hungry!"

After tasting a bit of York chocolate we follow Tom's advice and head out into the Yorkshire countryside. We find that North Yorkshire is vast, the biggest county in the UK, with two picturesque National Parks, the North York Moors and the Yorkshire Dales. First, we explore the high, broad North York Moors. Hawks soar above pine forests, which look great for den-building. Grouse and pheasants hide among clumps of bracken and purple heather, with good reason. In the Autumn--the shooting season--Tom's grandad will come up here with his flat cap, his dog and his gun, to see how many birds he can 'bag'. Leaving the moors, we travel west and go down and then up again: down into the flat Vale of York, where we pass several ruined castles and abbeys, and then up again into hills with a very different character. These are the Yorkshire Dales, which are part of the Pennines, the backbone of England. Wide valleys like Swaledale and Wensleydale are full of sheep, which graze in traditional pastures enclosed by grey

drystone walls. Travelling further and higher, the lanes get narrower and the landscape gets bleaker. We pass outcrops of limestone and the scars of former lead mines. We hear the warbling calls of curlews, wading birds with curious curved beaks. In the winter these high hills are often covered with snow and remote village communities can be cut off for days.

Further south, we come down from the hilltops to see several large towns and cities spreading out before us: Halifax, Huddersfield, Bradford and Leeds. The valleys of West and South Yorkshire were the perfect location for cloth factories in the Industrial Revolution, as there was plenty of local wool, coal and fast-flowing water, and the rivers could carry boat-loads of goods away to be sold. These characterful towns, nestled among the steep hills, grew quickly during the nineteenth century, but in the twentieth many factories closed. Leeds is now a thriving modern city, particularly in finance. Sheffield still produces some steel but the coal mines have all closed in the region and this has led to lots of jobs being lost and poverty in some towns.

The East Riding of Yorkshire, to the east of York, is totally different again. Large flat fields are full of yellow corn or dotted with pig sties, and criss-crossed by green hedgerows. Then, seemingly out of nowhere, chalk hills rise steeply up from the plain. These are the Yorkshire wolds, whose white chalky paths and rolling grassy slopes remind us of the South Downs, which we encountered hundreds of miles away in South East England. At the coast there are so many things to see, from lighthouses to sandy beaches to seabirds nesting on cliffs. Our final stop is the port city of Hull, near the mouth of the River Humber. Standing by the docks, we imagine all the trading ships and invading ships that have gone in and out of this estuary, as well as countless thousands of fishing boats. Now, the estuary is spanned by the huge Humber suspension bridge, the longest in the UK. But instead of lingering at the dock, we investigate the seas for ourselves at The Deep. This is an aquarium which helps to protect marine animals through conservation projects, and we enjoy close encounters with sharks, stingrays, penguins and tropical fish.

North West England
N
SCOTLAND
THE NORTH EAST
Carlisle
Solway Firth
Hadrian's Wall
CUMBRIA
R. Eden
Lake District
R. Lune
PENNINES
IRISH SEA
YORKSHIRE
Lancaster
Morecambe Bay
LANCASHIRE
R. Ribble
Red Rose of Lancaster
Preston
Manchester
Liverpool
R. Mersey
Manchester Ship Canal
CHESHIRE
Chester
WALES

chapter 16

North West England

From Yorkshire, let us head westward, right up over the Pennines, and on the other side we will find the county of Lancashire. In the Middle Ages a long battle, the Wars of the Roses, was fought between the royal House of York, whose badge had a white rose, and the House of Lancaster, whose emblem was a red rose. The wars finally ended, and the two houses were united, when Lancastrian Henry VII married the Yorkist princess Elizabeth in 1486. Their new badge was the red and white 'Tudor rose', but the counties of Yorkshire and Lancashire have never forgotten their history and to this day there is a good-humoured rivalry between their people. Large parts of Lancashire are rural, and farming communities live in the hillsides of the western Pennines and the Forest of Bowland and beside the rivers Lune and Ribble. There is a local saying, about a local hill, "If you can see Pendle Hill, it's about to rain. If you can't see Pendle Hill, it's already raining." Like much of western Britain, there is no shortage of rain here to water the lush grass, which feeds the many sheep and cattle. Cows are also abundant further south, on the flat meadows of the Cheshire plain. In Roman times, the small city of Chester

was the largest fortress in Britain. We can still see the remains of an amphitheatre and bath house, and Chester has kept its original Roman street layout, with main roads heading North, East, South and West from a central cross, surrounded by a thick defensive wall. Other buildings are made of local red bricks or 'half-timbered' with black and white frontages, and there are some unusual shops, called The Rows. The upper storey, or row, of shops sticks out and overhangs the shops on ground level, so you can walk along the sheltered gallery on a rainy day without getting wet.

Between Cheshire and Lancashire lies one of the biggest urban areas in the British Isles. The cities of Liverpool and Manchester played an important role in the Industrial Revolution, when they grew quickly and merged with several nearby towns. Manchester and its surrounding area had hundreds of factories, busily spinning and weaving most of the world's cotton. The cotton cloth was taken to nearby Liverpool, where it was exported overseas. Liverpool still has one of the biggest ports in Britain, where the River Mersey meets the Irish Sea. Along the waterfront we can see many beautiful port buildings, and a cruise ship which is about to dock. People from Liverpool, known as Liverpudlians, speak with a distinctive accent known as 'Scouse'. In modern times, Liverpool has become well known for its football club and its pop music, including the world-famous Beatles. From Liverpool, let's follow the Manchester Ship Canal inland to the Salford Quays, at Manchester. Gleaming modern buildings house hundreds of businesses and offices, and part of the quayside is called MediaCityUK. Here we meet a local family, Alessia, Rafael and Mia, and their mum. They are descended from Italian families who moved to Manchester during the nineteenth century, and made a living making and selling ice cream! They live nearby and Alessia, who wants to be an actress, loves coming to the MediaCity and spotting the people who work here in the BBC's northern headquarters. Her brother and sister are much more interested in the vast football stadium just across the canal, Old Trafford, the home of Manchester United. "Man United is the best team in the world!" they tell us. They follow every match, men's and women's, and save

MEDIACITY, MANCHESTER

up their pocket money to buy the kit.

We all catch a tram together into the city centre and walk along bustling streets, between Victorian red brick buildings and modern skyscrapers. Like other cities, Manchester has problems of crime, graffiti and homelessness, as well as opportunities to make things better. Alessia and her family point out 'The Green Building', which was designed to be environmentally friendly, there are bike bays instead of car parking spaces, water is heated by solar power, and there are no baths, only showers, to encourage people to use less water. We walk under a beautiful red and golden gate which marks the entrance to Chinatown, and see lots of Chinese people. Many of them are students at the university, and they are buying Chinese food from the cafes and supermarkets. We stop to pick up a takeaway meal with rice and noodles, before saying goodbye to Alessia and her family. They have encouraged us, while we are in the North West, to visit the Lake District, so that will be our next stop. This region has lots of motorways but, inspired by the Green Building to choose an environmentally-friendly option, we decide to travel by train. We pass through the busy Manchester Piccadilly station, and we're off.

It isn't long before we really feel like we've left the hustle and bustle behind us. Through the train window we see many fields, the busy town of Preston and the historic castle at Lancaster. As we approach the Lake District itself it's a bit like entering a different land. The peaks of the hills here are much steeper and higher than anything we remember seeing further south, and the lakes themselves are wide, serene and beautiful. There are certainly plenty of tourists here, staying in campsites, cottages or B&Bs, but once we strike a path up into the hills--or 'fells' as they are known here--it is peaceful and quiet. We can see why poets like William Wordsworth were inspired by this landscape! Beatrix Potter lived here, farming the local Herdwick breed of sheep, and writing stories about the woodland animals. She was so keen to conserve the beauty of this place that she worked closely with the founders of the National Trust, a charity that now looks after large swathes of coastline and countryside across the UK.

If we were to travel further north still, we would approach the border with Scotland, and find the town of Carlisle. We would see ruined castles nestled among the hillsides, evidence of this region's turbulent history, poised as it is between two nations, which were not always at peace. But let's wait and explore these properly in the next chapter, when we move into the North East. In the meantime, we'll climb another hill, and munch some lakeland gingerbread while we enjoy the view.

Ullswater, in the Lake District

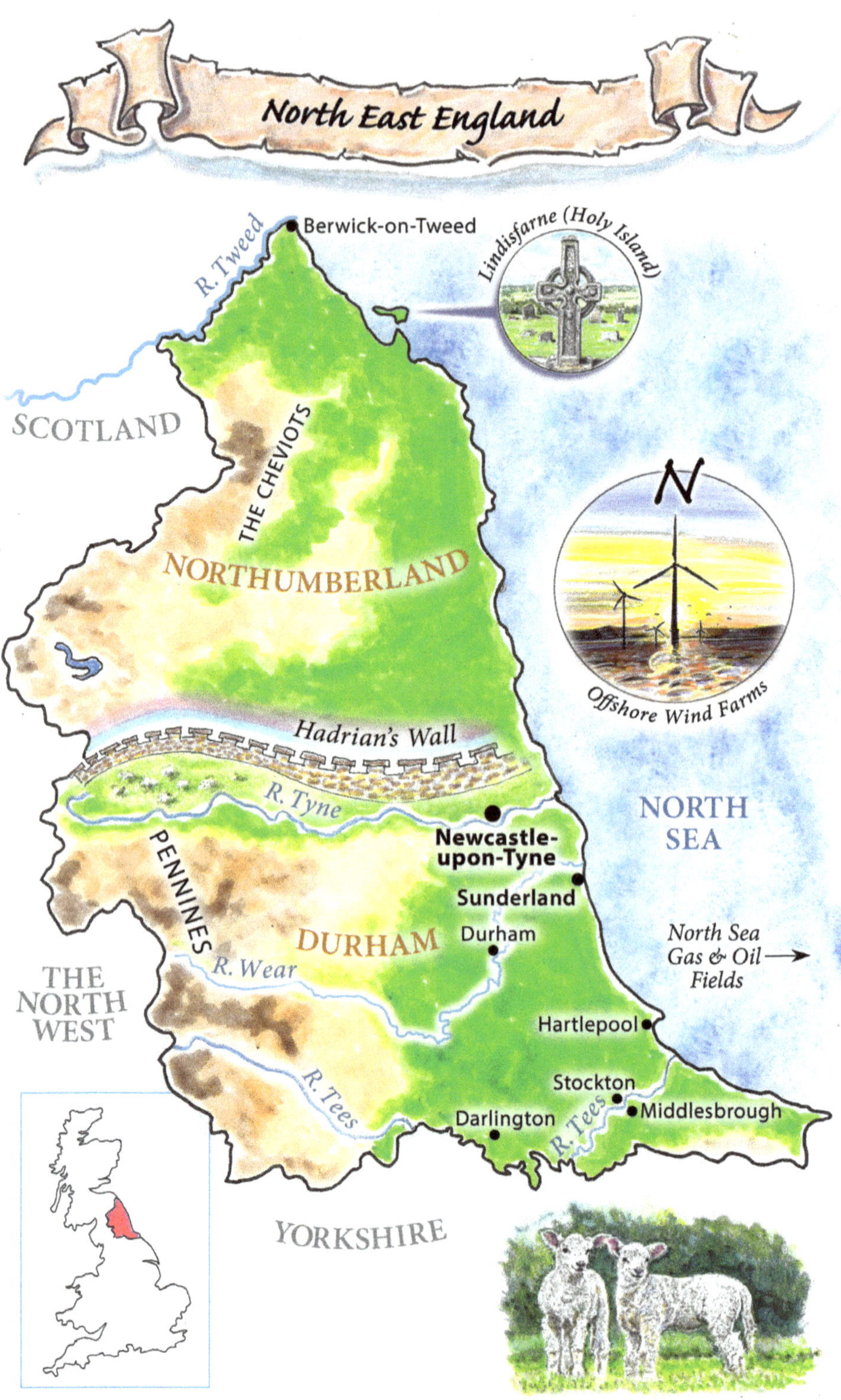

North East England
Berwick-on-Tweed
R. Tweed
Lindisfarne (Holy Island)
SCOTLAND
THE CHEVIOTS
NORTHUMBERLAND
N
Offshore Wind Farms
Hadrian's Wall
R. Tyne
PENNINES
NORTH SEA
Newcastle-upon-Tyne
Sunderland
DURHAM
Durham
THE NORTH WEST
R. Wear
North Sea Gas & Oil Fields
Hartlepool
R. Tees
Stockton
Darlington
R. Tees
Middlesbrough
YORKSHIRE

chapter 17

North East England

As WE EXPLORE the north-east of England, the first thing that strikes us is a great and ancient wall, with ruined towers and fortresses, stretching from west to east as far as the eye can see. Who built this wall, and why? Two thousand years ago, the Romans invaded Britain and conquered the land all the way from the south coast to the land we now call northern England. Here they were resisted by the Picts, the 'painted people', who lived in what we now call Scotland. The Emperor Hadrian wanted to defend his mighty Roman Empire, so he ordered that a great wall should be built along the frontier. Hadrian's Wall crossed the whole country, from shore to shore, and much of it can still be seen today. Further north-east, the English county of Northumberland has countless castles in various states of ruin or repair, whose bricks tell tales of the strife between the English and the Scots throughout the Middle Ages.

These walls and castles are great places to imagine a bygone or mythical age, to play kings and queens, knights and princesses, fairies and warriors and dragons. We can climb the large, rounded Cheviot Hills and seek out the wild goats and Iron Age hill forts at the top. After that we can enjoy the long sandy beaches by the sea, get on a boat to see the seals and puffins on the Farne Islands, or cross the causeway to Holy Island at Lindisfarne. After dark, we find that the night sky is darker here than anywhere else in the country, so it is perfect for stargazing. By contrast, most of England has so many electric lights from buildings and roads that 'light pollution' can affect our view of the sky. In Northumberland we can see thousands of stars, the Milky Way and even the Andromeda Galaxy, which is more than two million light years away!

Making our way back to Hadrian's Wall, we follow it to its eastern end and find a bustling city called Newcastle, on the River Tyne, close to the North Sea. It is named after the city's 'new' castle, which was built by the son of William the Conqueror. That was in 1080, so it is now nearly a thousand years old, but it was new once! The people who live in and around Newcastle are known as 'Geordies' and their way of speaking,

Hadrian's Wall

their accent and dialect, is very distinctive. It is thought the name 'Geordie' comes from the city's support for King George II instead of the Jacobite Bonnie Prince Charlie in 1745, as well as the lamps designed by George 'Geordie' Stephenson that were used in the many coal mines. The land around Newcastle was famous for coal mining and ship-building, and ships would sail from Newcastle to London, laden with coal to fuel its factories. There was so much coal heading out of Newcastle, that people used to joke that if you 'take coals to Newcastle' you are doing something pointless! The coal mines have closed now, but there are still plenty of people involved in getting fuel out of the ground. In fact, for some families, their dads are only at home some of the time, because their work lies far, far out to sea. Let me explain.

In the 1960s and 70s, huge underground lakes, or reservoirs, of oil were discovered, under the seabed of the North Sea. Oil can be drilled from these reservoirs and piped up to platforms, or rigs, which stand on great tall stilts above the waves, in the middle of the sea. The oil is processed and then sent through a long pipe that lies on the sea bed, all the way to shore, 200 miles away. The men working on oil rigs are flown there by helicopter and usually work for two weeks on the rig, then have two weeks at home with their families, and so on. Would you like to work for two weeks away, and then have a two-week holiday?

Natural gas is also taken from under the North Sea. If you have a gas cooker or central heating in your house, perhaps that gas came from under the North Sea! Gas and oil, along with coal, are known as fossil fuels, and they are used for generating electricity, powering cars and making all sorts of things.

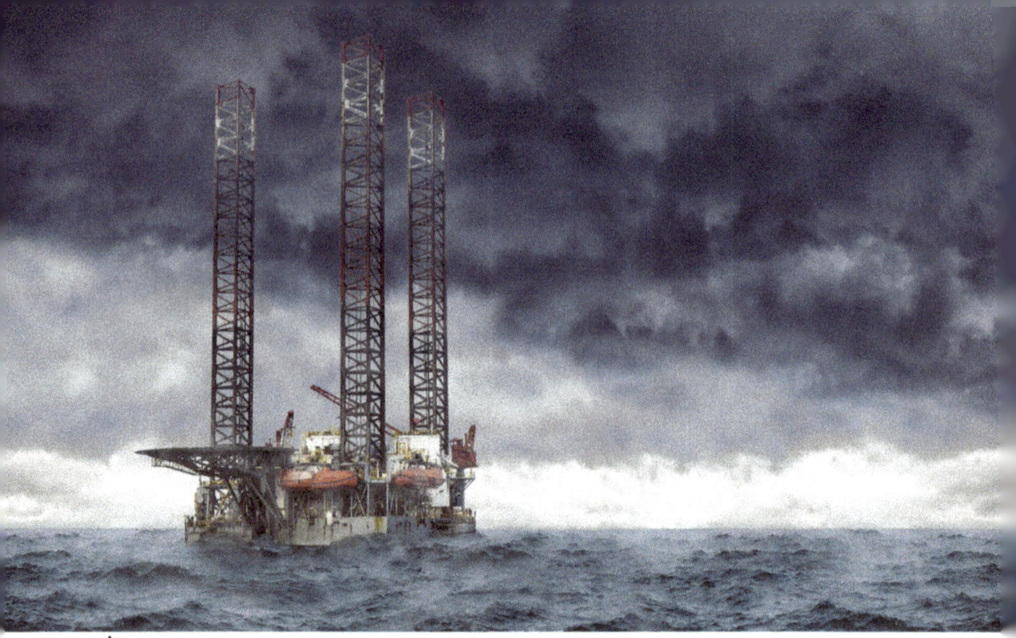

AN OIL RIG ON THE NORTH SEA

There are lots of factories in the North East, particularly near a town called Middlesbrough, which uses oil to make plastics, chemicals and fertilisers. Unfortunately, burning fossil fuels also makes harmful gases, such as carbon dioxide, and these lead to climate warming and other environmental and health hazards. Because of this, more and more people are trying to use cleaner and also renewable energy instead, getting power from the wind and sun through wind turbines and solar panels. When there are lots of wind turbines together it is called a wind farm, and the largest wind farm in the world is being built here in the North Sea. Electricity is also generated by nuclear power plants, including one here in Hartlepool, on

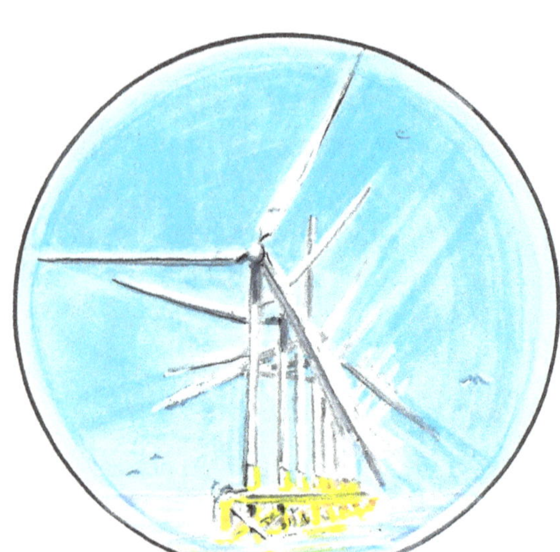

the North East coast. Nearby, at Sunderland, a huge Nissan car factory produces electric cars alongside petrol cars.

Our tour of the North East would not be complete without a trip to the historic city of Durham. The magnificent Norman cathedral and castle, which is now part of the famous Durham University, stand high above the River Wear, and overlook the town. County Durham is also notable for being the birthplace of rail travel. The Stockton and Darlington Railway carried the first railway passengers in the world in 1825, using a steam engine made by the inventor George Stephenson. From here, railways have spread all over the country and all over the world. Let us appreciate George Stephenson's legacy by hopping on a train from Durham that will take us northwards, through Newcastle, along the Northumbrian coast, and all the way to Scotland.

WIND FARMS OFF THE NORTH SEA

Scotland - The Lowlands
HIGHLAND SCOTLAND
R. Tay
Arbroath
Dundee
Firth of Tay
Perth
St. Andrews
Stirling
Firth of Forth
CENTRAL LOWLANDS
Glasgow
Forth Bridge
Edinburgh
Berwick-upon-Tweed
R. Clyde
Firth of Clyde
R. Tweed
N
Jedburgh
SOUTHERN UPLANDS
THE BORDERS
Dumfries
Solway Firth
ENGLAND

chapter 18

Scotland - the Lowlands

THE SOUTHERN PART of Scotland is called the Scottish Lowlands, especially around the central part between Edinburgh and Glasgow. Not all the land is flat, for it rolls with many hills particularly towards the border with England, an area known as the Southern Uplands. However, the landscape as a whole is lower than the mountainous Highlands in the north and west. The plentiful rain and gentle pastures in regions such as Ayrshire in the south-west are suitable for grazing dairy cows, while in the east large fields are planted with oats, barley and potatoes. Oats are made into porridge, the stomach-warming breakfast food, for which Scotland is famous. Soft fruit like strawberries grow here in abundance, protected from the cold by long plastic covers called polytunnels. A famous breed of black cattle, Aberdeen Angus, came originally from eastern Scotland, and is now farmed across the world for its tasty beef. Most of Scotland's larger towns and cities are found in the Lowlands, from Dumfries in the south, to the major cities of Edinburgh and Glasgow, as well as Stirling, Perth and Dundee. St Andrew's is a historic town on the east coast and is home to Scotland's oldest university and

A DELICIOUS BOWL OF SCOTTISH PORRIDGE WITH MILK AND BUTTER

a famous golf club. Let us continue our train journey and visit some of these places.

The train that we boarded in north-east England passes into the hilly region known as the Scottish Borders. Jedburgh and Roxburgh were important border towns in the medieval battles between Scotland and England. These turbulent times turned many local families into lawless robbers called 'Reivers'. Reivers held grudges against other families or 'clans', and they would burn down each other's towers and steal their cattle. Their legacy can still be seen in the many ruined Reiver towers in this area, and in the family names that continue to this day. In fact, if your surname is Armstrong, Bell, Scott, Graham or Maxwell, you might be related to these fearsome pillagers! Thankfully the land is now peaceful and prosperous and our train route takes us safely along the east coast of Scotland. We can look out over the North Sea as we make our way towards the capital city, Edinburgh.

There is so much to explore in Edinburgh, we hardly know where to start. Our attention is caught first by Edinburgh Castle, which stands high on a rocky cliff overlooking the city. At the other end of an ancient road called the Royal Mile is the Palace of Holyroodhouse. When it was built, five hundred years ago, lions, tigers and bears were kept in the gardens! Now the gardens are used for the Queen's Garden Parties, which host 8,000 guests, and serve 15,000 cups of tea and 9,000 jam tarts. Nearby is a great extinct volcano called Arthur's Seat, and if we climb to the top, we can see the city stretching before us. Alongside the modern buildings, the city centre has two main parts: the medieval Old Town, with crowded cobbled alleys, and the Georgian New Town, which was carefully planned in the eighteenth century. In the distance we see the docks and the hills. Edinburgh is always busy with the many people who live here, working for example in the banks and insurance companies, in medical research, or catering for millions of tourists. At certain times of the year, though, special events fill the city with greater crowds and excitement. In the summer there is a famous arts festival, in which the streets and theatres come alive with music and drama. On New Year's Eve, known here as Hogmanay, there

EDINBURGH, CAPITAL OF SCOTLAND

are spectacular fireworks. On 25th January, people all over Scotland celebrate the birthday of one of their favourite poets, Robert Burns. They have fun reciting Burns' poems and eating haggis, a national dish made from sheep's offal. The haggis is traditionally carried to the table while somebody plays the bagpipes, a Scottish musical instrument. The host performs Burns' poem 'Address to a Haggis' before the meal is eaten. Another local specialty is the delicious Edinburgh rock, a soft crumbly sweet that comes in lots of different colours.

We hop back on the train to visit another city, Glasgow, one hour away. Edinburgh may be the capital of Scotland, but Glasgow is the biggest city, and there are all sorts of museums, galleries, parks and theatres we could visit. We make our way to the River Clyde, and find a tall sailing ship moored there. Venturing on board, we explore the whole ship, from the captain's cabin to the cargo hold, we ring the ship's bell and turn the wheel. A man dressed as First Mate tells us that local children sometimes have birthday parties here! The ship was

GLASGOW CITY

built right here on the banks of the Clyde over 120 years ago, and sailed around the world. In fact, the area around Glasgow was one of the busiest centres for shipbuilding in the world, along with coal mining and steel making. Now there are a whole range of industries, from brewing beer to making satellites, and such a lot of people are involved in electronics that the centre of Scotland is known as Silicon Glen, like the Silicon Valley in California.

From Glasgow we could travel south into Dumfries and Galloway to look for red squirrels in the pine forests or ospreys catching fish in the quiet lochs. Instead, we travel north-east across the green countryside, passing castle after castle, until we reach Dundee. Dundee is Scotland's fourth largest city and it sits beside the wide inlet called the Firth of Tay. Moored in the dock is the Royal Research Ship (RRS) *Discovery*, which was built here in Dundee over a hundred years ago. This is the ship in which Captain Scott and his intrepid crew set out on

an ill-fated quest to reach the South Pole. The shipbuilders of Dundee had a long tradition of making ships for the Arctic whaling trade, so they were an ideal choice to build a ship destined to travel to the icy Antarctic. Dundee still contributes to important scientific and medical research in its universities and hospitals. It also produces famous Dundee cake and marmalade, which we must taste while we are here!

Just a few miles from Dundee, we find a large ruined church near the North Sea. This is Arbroath Abbey, and it is a significant place for many Scots who would like to be independent from the United Kingdom. Let's find out their story.

In the medieval period, Scotland and England were separate kingdoms, and the kings of Scotland were always crowned on a special stone called the Stone of Scone, or 'Stone of Destiny'. However, the kings of England claimed that they should rule Scotland. In 1296, English King Edward I won some battles and boldly took the Stone of Scone away. In 1320 a group of

Scottish barons gathered here at Arbroath Abbey to appeal for help from the Pope. They wrote the 'Declaration of Arbroath' claiming that "it is in truth not for glory, nor riches, nor honours that we are fighting, but for freedom." But Scotland and England continued to battle each other for hundreds of years. In 1603, England's Queen Elizabeth I died without an heir and the Scottish King James VI became king of England and Scotland. Still, however, the Stone of Scone was kept in London, at Westminster Abbey. There it remained until, on Christmas Day 1950, it was stolen! It mysteriously reappeared here at Arbroath Abbey, draped in the national flag of Scotland. It had been taken by Scottish nationalists who, like those barons so many centuries earlier, wanted independence. The Stone of Scone was formally given back to Scotland in 1996 and it is now held safely in Edinburgh Castle. The question of whether Scotland should be an independent country is still debated by many people throughout the United Kingdom.

THE STONE OF SCONE

Scotland - The Highlands
N
ATLANTIC OCEAN
Shetland Pony
Orkney Islands
Cape Wrath
John o' Groats
approx. 258 km NE of The Orkneys
Outer Hebrides
Skye
Shetland Islands
Moray Firth
THE GREAT GLEN
Inverness
Inner Hebrides
L. Ness
R. Spey
CAIRNGORMS
Aberdeen
Glenfinnan
GRAMPIANS
R. Dee
Fort William
Ben Nevis
L. Lomond
NORTH SEA
LOWLAND SCOTLAND

Scotland – the Highlands

WE CONTINUE NORTHWARDS, ready to explore the glorious Highlands of Scotland. The Highlands are beautiful with unspoilt natural scenery and majestic mountains. The land has thin or peaty soil and, where rain is blown in from the Atlantic Ocean on the west, wet weather. The mountains and valleys, in addition to being high and steep, are relatively hard to reach because they are at the farthest extreme of the island of Britain, and include many remote islands to the north and west. These aspects of landscape and climate have affected the farming, work and traditions that developed over hundreds of years, and still shape the communities to this day. Travelling north along the eastern seaboard, we arrive at Aberdeen, the city known as Gateway to the Highlands. Stately grey granite buildings line the route to the port, which bustles with fishing vessels and boats that support the North Sea oil industry. People also enjoy surfing and paddle-boarding at the sandy beaches, or fishing for salmon or brown trout in the River Dee. Out at sea, fishing boats catch cod, haddock, herring, mackerel and shellfish. Not far inland lie the mighty Cairngorm Mountains, which are home to elusive mountain hares and pine martens, herds of red deer and even reindeer. Ancient Scots pine trees grow in the valleys, keeping their green needles all winter, while on the rounded mountain tops hardy birds called ptarmigan grow white feathers to camouflage themselves against the winter snow.

Travelling westwards, we reach Inverness, 'The Capital of the Highlands'. Here we meet a girl called Isla, who wants to be a marine biologist. She has been inspired to love sea creatures by watching the pods of bottlenose dolphins that live in the Moray Firth, just outside Inverness. "I went on a whale-watching trip last summer and even saw a minke whale!" she tells us. "I'd love to go to the Orkneys and see the orca up there." Orca, or killer whales, often swim past the Orkney Islands, which lie to the north of Scotland's north coast. Beyond the Orkneys are the Shetland Islands, and then there is no more land until you reach the Arctic! These islands are so far north that in midsummer it stays light all night, but in midwinter the dim sun sets early over the crofters' cottages. Back in Inverness, Isla shows us round the Botanic Gardens, the Cathedral and the Castle, which is where fateful events happened in Shakespeare's 'Scottish Play', Macbeth. Outside Inverness there are ancient standing stones and burial chambers, known as 'cairns', which were built in the Bronze

Dolphins in the Moray Firth

Age, over 5,000 years ago. But Isla's favourite local attraction is Loch Ness, with its mythical monster, 'Nessie'. "The waters of Loch Ness are so deep and mysterious," Isla says. "I'm sure Nessie is down there somewhere, we just haven't seen him yet!"

Loch Ness is long, narrow and picturesque, framed by steep mountain slopes and the atmospheric remains of Urquhart Castle. It lies in a long, straight valley called the Great Glen, which follows a natural faultline in the ground beneath. The Great Glen slices all the way through northern Scotland from coast to coast. We can travel the whole length of the Great Glen by boat, and this gives us time to admire the scenery. Many of the hills and mountains have steep sides and thin soil so they are not suitable for growing crops. Instead, they are grazed by varieties of sheep and cattle that are good at foraging and can cope with the cold weather. Highland cows have long horns and shaggy auburn hair which flops over their eyes and keeps them warm in the long, cold and wet Highland winters. One business that does flourish in the Highlands, using the peaty water is the making of Whisky, a strong drink exported all over the world.

At the far end of the Great Glen we find the town of Fort William, where Isla's cousin Finlay lives. Finlay loves being outdoors. His parents run an outdoor activity centre for tourists, so he has plenty of opportunities to enjoy canoeing, mountain biking and skiing when he's not in school. "People come here to Fort William from all over Scotland and England, and Europe and America too," he tells us. "Some of them are just passing through on their way to the islands, but some want to climb Ben Nevis, up there." He points to the giant of a mountain, Britain's tallest, which rises behind us with its head in the clouds. From Fort William, the Road to the Isles takes travellers through beautiful mountain scenery to the west coast, where passengers can board ferries to the islands of Rum, Eigg and Skye. The Small Isles, Inner Hebrides and Outer Hebrides are some of the remotest parts of the British Isles. Much of the north-western mainland is equally difficult to reach because steep sea lochs cut sharply into the land. This remoteness makes it a haven for wildlife and for travellers who want to enjoy the unspoilt wilderness. Many salmon farms have also become established here, in which young fish live in freshwater tanks beside the lochs, while the adults swim in huge netted pens in the coastal seawater.

"I've been to the Isle of Skye a few times," Finlay says. "It's great because lots of people there speak Gaelic." Finlay goes to a Gaelic school, which means all his lessons are in Gaelic, the Celtic language which has been spoken by Highland families, or 'clans', for hundreds of years. Finlay enjoys other Highland traditions too, he has a tartan kilt, is learning to play the bagpipes, and loves going to the Glenfinnan Highland Games. At the games you can see traditional Highland dancing and piping, and competitors test their strength by playing tug-of-war and tossing the 'caber', a heavy wooden pole.

It was here at Glenfinnan that many Highland clansmen joined the exiled Charles Edward Stuart, or 'Bonnie Prince Charlie', in

THE HIGHLAND GAMES

1745. The Highlanders fought for the Jacobite cause, longing for the Stuarts, the old Scottish kings, to rule instead of King George II. They were defeated, and for a while Highland customs like wearing tartan and playing bagpipes were outlawed. Glenfinnan is also famous for another reason. Finlay points out the tall arches of a viaduct, a railway bridge poised between the mountain slopes, which is crossed by the 'Jacobite' steam train. Many train enthusiasts and Harry Potter fans enjoy seeing this, as it was the film location for the railway to Hogwarts, and the books themselves were written in Edinburgh. We say goodbye to Finlay and catch a train heading south. Our final stop is at Loch Lomond in the Trossachs National Park, which lies between the Highlands and Lowlands. Here we can enjoy some watersports on the loch or cycle among the trees. We don't want to get bitten by midges, so we wear long sleeves as we pitch our tents, and experience wild camping under the starry sky.

Wales
ENGLAND
Liverpool
Menai Bridge
Pontcysyllte Aqueduct
Isle of Anglesey
Colwyn Bay
Caernarfon
Mt. Snowdon
Porthmadog
R. Dee
Lake Vrnwy
Lyn Peninsula
CAMBRIANS
R. Severn
IRISH SEA
R. Wye
Cardigan Bay
R. Severn
St. David's
PEMBROKESHIRE
BRECON BEACONS
R. Usk
Swansea
Newport
Port Talbot
Gower Peninsula
Cardiff
Bristol Channel
N
zzzzz...

chapter 20

Wales

WALES IS ONE of the four nations which have joined to make the United Kingdom. It is a small country, sticking out into the Irish Sea to the west of England, but it has strong traditions and a proud identity of its own. If a Welsh person outside Wales detects the lilting Welsh accent when they meet a stranger, they immediately talk about where they are from and enjoy sharing their favourite things about Wales. Perhaps they love rugby, or the Celtic myths about red dragons slumbering on the mountaintops. Their favourite snack might be welsh cakes or bara brith. Bara brith, which means 'speckled bread' is a tea loaf speckled with dried fruit and is a teatime treat in many homes. They might celebrate St David's Day on 1st March by pinning a leek or daffodil, symbols of Wales, to their clothes. St David was the patron saint of Wales, and his day is a festival for Welsh traditions every year. As children, they might have worn traditional Welsh costume to school on this day and performed in the school choir or poetry recitals. Special chapel services would include songs written by Welsh hymn-writers and for dinner they might have eaten traditional favourites like cawl, a soup made from leeks, or tasty roast lamb. In the

bigger towns and cities, they might have seen large parades and festivals of poetry and music known as Eisteddfod. Let's take a tour around this characterful country and see what else we can find out about Wales.

The mountainous heartland of central Wales is rural, rugged, and beautiful. Flocks of sheep graze on the grassy hillsides of the Brecon Beacons, while polecats and otters hide among the forests and marshes, streams and waterfalls of the Cambrian Mountains. In the past mining for metals such as copper and iron and quarrying for slate led to the construction of a canal to carry these heavy goods and resulted in the amazing Pontcysyllte Aqueduct. Emerging from the hills of mid Wales, trickling streams grow to become the impressive rivers Severn and Wye, which flow through eastern Wales and western England before feeding into the Bristol Channel. Several large reservoirs, which were built to provide water for English cities like Liverpool and Birmingham, now also provide a home for birds like grebes and ospreys. Lake Vyrnwy is one of the biggest of these. Further north are the rocky peaks of Snowdonia. Here crows with red beaks, called choughs, nest on cliff tops, and peregrine falcons dart like a bullet through the skies, proving themselves to be the fastest bird in the world. Many humans also enjoy exploring these craggy slopes, and the bravest enjoy rock climbing or bouldering, which is rock climbing without any ropes or harnesses! These remote landscapes are unspoilt by buildings, traffic or pollution. There are very few roads across the hills and not many people live in this region, but most of those who do, speak Welsh and enjoy keeping Welsh traditions alive. As we travel through Wales we see that Welsh and English are the two national languages, and all the road signs have everything written twice, once in Welsh and once in English. At one time people were worried that the Welsh language would die out, but now it is becoming more and more popular to learn Welsh, and many children to go to Welsh-speaking schools.

Leaving the high slopes of the highest mountain, Mount Snowdon, behind us, we reach the north-west coast of Wales, and cross the bridge to the island of Anglesey. This is the largest island in England and Wales, and when the Romans arrived in Britain, they found that Anglesey was a stronghold

Mount Snowdon

of the Celtic Britons and their priests, the Druids. After two invasions, the Romans eventually conquered Anglesey, which became the western frontier of the Roman Empire. They dug copper from the Anglesey's copper mines and built a mighty fort on the Welsh mainland. More than a thousand years later, the stones from the fort were rebuilt into a new castle, Caernarfon Castle, by another invader, Edward I. Edward was an English king who wanted to rule Wales as well, and brought a large army to defeat the last Welsh prince, Llewelyn ap Gruffudd. After his victory, Edward built many impressive castles throughout Wales which can still be seen and visited today.

The Welsh coast has many treasures. In the north, holiday-makers love to visit the sandy beaches, piers and promenades of seaside towns such as Colwyn Bay and Llandudno. In the west, the harbour town of Porthmadog has a curious, man-made island, formed out of rocks from all over the world.

CAERNARFON CASTLE

How did they get here? Ships would set sail from Porthmadog full of slate from nearby slate mines to trade with people in different countries. On their return journey, they used local rocks as ballast, which weighed the ships down so that they didn't capsize in strong winds. When the ships arrived back at Porthmadog, the rocks from faraway countries were dumped in the harbour, in a pile that grew and grew, until it became a unique island. The natural beauties of the Welsh coast can be seen in the rocky cliffs and sheltered beaches of the Llyn peninsula in the north-west, Pembrokeshire in the south-west, and the Gower peninsula in the south. Exploring these coves, we can pick shells out of the rockpools, feel sand between our toes and watch seals bobbing in the water.

Eventually we head away from the coastal paths, and discover several large towns and cities in south Wales: Cardiff, Swansea, Port Talbot and Newport. There are more people living in this area than in any other part of Wales. One of the main reasons for this is hidden under the ground, where the South Wales Coalfield lies below the hills and valleys. During

the Industrial Revolution in the eighteenth and nineteenth centuries, crowds of people moved here from all over Wales and other countries. They worked in the coal pits, or transporting coal to ports like Cardiff, and from there to the rest of the world. The coal pits have closed now, but we can find out what it would have been like for the miners by visiting the many museums that celebrate this heritage. We can see the terraced houses in which they lived, and travel deep down the mine shafts wearing helmets and head torches! Back at ground level, we can explore Cardiff.

Cardiff is the capital city of Wales and is also its centre for business and financial activities. It is next to the sea and has a large bay, surrounded by a nature reserve, sports village, restaurants, parks and the Senedd. The Senedd is the Welsh Parliament, where politicians make laws affecting, for example, Welsh schools, hospitals and the environment. Just like the parliaments in England, Scotland and Northern Ireland, anyone can visit, and watch and listen to the debates from the public gallery. Afterwards, visitors can go to the café and enjoy a cup of tea and a Welsh cake, which is like a cross between a pancake and a scone. Delicious!

Outside the cafe are lots of rugby fans with red scarves, singing songs and celebrating a Welsh victory against the English. The Welsh love rugby.

RUGBY BALL

WELSH CAKES

Ireland
N
ATLANTIC OCEAN
Malin Head
Giant's Causeway
NORTHERN IRELAND
Londonderry/ Derry
DONEGAL
ULSTER
L. Neagh
Donegal
Belfast
Slieve League Cliffs
SPERRIN MTNS.
L. Erne
Armagh
MOURNE MTNS.
Slieve Donard
Croagh Patrick
CONNACHT
CAVAN
R. Shannon
LEINSTER
L. Ree
R. Boyne
L. Corrib
R. Liffey
Doolin Cave
L. Derg
WESTMEATH
Dublin
IRISH SEA
Aran Islands
Grand Canal
Cliffs of Moher
OFFALY
R. Barrow
WICKLOW MTNS
CLARE
R. Shannon
LAOIS
Limerick
TIPPERARY
MUNSTER
KERRY
Dingle
Mount Carrauntoohil
CORK
Cork
R. Lee
REPUBLIC OF IRELAND (ÈIRE)
Mizen Head

Northern Ireland

ACROSS THE IRISH SEA, in the north-eastern part of the island of Ireland, we find Northern Ireland. It is formed from six of the nine counties of a historic Irish province called Ulster. Although it is on the same island as the Republic of Ireland, we remember that Northern Ireland is part of the United Kingdom. It is a green and fertile land, with mild temperatures and plenty of rain throughout the year. The abundant green grass supports cows, sheep, poultry and pigs, which are mostly raised on small, family-run farms. There are a few cities, like Belfast which is the capital and Armagh - which unusually has two St Patrick's Cathedrals! But most of the landscape is rural with many small market-towns.

Lough Neagh, which is the largest lake in the British Isles, sits at the centre of a large bowl of land, with green hills and mountains rising on almost all sides. On the shores of Lough Neagh are several nature reserves, which shelter red and grey squirrels, cuckoos, butterflies, lizards and many water birds. The habitats include conifer forests and broad-leaved forests, peat bogs and drumlins. Drumlins are curious oval-shaped hills, thought to have been created by retreating ice age gla-

ciers. One of the most striking landscape features of Northern Ireland is the Giants' Causeway on the northern coastline. It is a vast pavement of about 40,000 hexagonal columns, made from a dark volcanic rock called basalt. The columns have flat tops and a fascinatingly regular, interconnected pattern. You can clamber over them and imagine giants striding into the waves, towards Scotland on the far side of the sea!

The true story of Northern Ireland has indeed been shaped by the many crossings over this short channel of sea which, at its narrowest, is only thirteen miles wide. Throughout history Celts, Vikings and Normans have come and gone across the sea between this north coast of Ireland and the rest of Britain, in order to trade, invade, spread learning or seek shelter. Scotland and Ireland share a Celtic heritage, including a Gaelic language and traditions such as bagpipes. As we have already heard, the monastery at Iona, off the west coast of Scotland, was founded by monks from Ireland in 563 AD. Ireland's history of monasteries and learning have led some to call it The Land of Saints and Scholars.' During the medieval period, the Norman kings of England began to control Ireland through invasions and alliances, and in the seventeenth century, lots of Protestant soldiers and farmers from England and Scotland went to live in the northern part of Ireland. Most Irish people kept their Catholic faith and their Gaelic traditions, but they were badly treated. The Protestant leaders did not let them share in ruling the country and many Irish had to leave their land. In 1688 Britain's Catholic king James II was deposed by William III 'of Orange'. Many Irish Catholics had supported James and his forces, the 'Jacobites', but William beat them at the Battle of the Boyne in 1690 and this victory is still celebrated by Protestants across Northern Ireland to this day. Every year on the 12th July, thousands of people take part in parades wearing bowler hats and orange sashes, and many more line the streets to see the banners and hear the drums and pipes of the marching bands. Their Catho-

THE GIANT'S CAUSEWAY

lic neighbours, however, often feel upset by these marches, because they celebrate the defeat and unfair treatment of their community. The divisions continue to be seen in the second largest city of the region, which is called Londonderry by the Protestants, and Derry by the Catholics.

In the twentieth century, much of Ireland became an independent country, but most people in the north wanted to keep their connection with Great Britain. Northern Ireland was created, joined by land to the rest of Ireland, but belonging to the United Kingdom. This history continues to have a big impact on people's lives in Northern Ireland. Many Protestants see themselves as part of the United Kingdom, whereas most Catholics see themselves as part of Ireland. This disagreement erupted into violence on the streets in 'the Troubles' of the late twentieth century, although thankfully, since the 'Good Friday Agreement' of 1998, there has been peace. Many people still have strong feelings about these issues, though, which affect where they live, which school the children go to and who

'HANDS ACROSS THE DIVIDE'

the adults vote for. In recent years, many cross-community projects and schools have been set up, which work to bring people together and move away from the divisions of the past.

Let's explore Belfast, the capital city, which has two universities, an international airport and a busy harbour. Many buildings have big pictures, called murals, painted on their walls, which show messages from 'the Troubles' as well as portraits of famous people and symbols of peace. Belfast City Hall is a grand building with great green domes made of copper. In front of the City Hall stands a statue of the nineteenth century British Queen Victoria, accompanied by statues representing the important trades of spinning and shipbuilding. During the Industrial Revolution, Belfast was famous for its linen-making, and even more famous for its shipbuilding, like the cities of Glasgow and Liverpool just across the sea. The most remarkable ship to have been designed and built here was the *RMS Titanic*. At the very place where she was launched, there is now a huge Titanic Experience museum. Visitors can explore the sights, sounds and smells of the biggest and most luxurious ship in the world, and then find out how she tragically sank after hitting an iceberg in 1912 on her very first voyage.

Outside Belfast there is a striking landscape to enjoy. Cave Hill is well known for its trails, Iron Age hill fort and, of course, dark caves. The outline of the hill looks like a sleeping giant, and it may have inspired the story of *Gulliver's Travels*, a book by Jonathan Swift, who lived near Belfast. In the story, a man called Gulliver is shipwrecked and wakes up on an island full of tiny people, so to them he looks like a sleeping giant. Nearby, Divis and Black Mountain are great places for dog walking, bike rides and picnics, and on a clear day you can get a fantastic view from the top. On one side you can look down over the city of Belfast and across the Irish Sea to Scotland and the Isle of Man. Down the coast, you can see in the distance the granite peaks of Northern Ireland's highest mountains, the Mourne mountains in County Down. Turning your gaze inland, you can look across the wide, round Lough Neagh, over the flat farmlands of the plain of Antrim, to the remote, heather-clad slopes of the Sperrin Mountains of County Tyrone.

chapter 22

Republic of Ireland

PART I

TRAVELLING SOUTH FROM Belfast, it is not long before we cross the border into a different country. As we noted before, the island of Ireland contains both Northern Ireland, which is part of the United Kingdom, and the Republic of Ireland, which is an independent country with its own government and laws. The republic's official name is Ireland, or Éire in Irish, so we will have to remember that 'Ireland' can either mean Ireland the island or Ireland the country! What a tongue-twister! There are many things that are common to the island of Ireland as a whole, such as its wet and mild weather all through the year. This creates such a green grassy landscape that its nickname is the Emerald Isle. You can imagine it as a beautiful green jewel surrounded by the blue Atlantic Ocean and Irish Sea. But that does not mean it is a small island, it is the second biggest island in Europe, after its neighbour Great Britain.

Throughout the island of Ireland, cows and sheep graze on the lush grassy slopes. Irish beef and butter, such as Kerrygold from County Cork, are famous and are exported to many other countries. Many sports have all-Irish teams with players from both Northern Ireland and the Republic of Ireland competing against other nations, for example in rugby, cricket and the Olympic Games. There is a strong sense of Irish history and identity across the island, and for many the Catholic faith and traditions are important. Some customs stretch back to their communities' Celtic past, and many people enjoy folk music and folk dancing, telling stories and telling jokes.

We reach Dublin, capital city of the Republic of Ireland. A quarter of Irish people live and work in and around this bustling city. We meet one of them, a girl called Cara. Her name means 'friend' in Irish and she offers to show us around. First, we head to the seafront. We can hear the squawking of gulls and we see many boats and ferries travelling in and out of the busy port.

"This is the east coast of Ireland," Cara tells us as we walk along the pier. "You can't see it from here, but across the sea there is Anglesey in North Wales, and beyond it, Liverpool in England. But the first people to build a town here in Dublin were actually Vikings from Norway. They had a king of Dublin called Olaf the White!"

Cara shows us the Dublinia museum, where children can dress up in Viking costume and write their name in runes, before exploring the sights and smells of medieval Dublin. "The English started taking over Ireland in the medieval times, and over the years the Irish people were treated badly, there were loads of battles and rebellions."

Continuing our tour of Dublin, Cara shows us long wide streets with grand buildings, including Trinity College and the General Post Office, GPO for short, with its tall, elegant

columns. "The GPO was the focus of the Easter Rising in 1916, where people fought for independence from the British. Look, you can still see bullet holes in the columns! And here is Leinster House, a rich duke used to live there, but now it's where the Oireachtas meets."

Oireachtas is the Irish word for parliament and Leinster House is a great white building. It looks a little like the White House, where the President of the United States of America lives, so we are not too surprised to find out the people who designed the White House were inspired by Leinster House. The Republic of Ireland has a President and a Prime Minister, a Senate and a House of Representatives, all elected by the people. Ireland is part of the European Union so its currency--or money--is the Euro. This means that Irish people go to the shops and buy things using Euro coins and notes, just like the people in France, Germany and many other European countries.

We keep walking and along the River Liffey there are lots of modern buildings made of glass. We see a huge new theatre, which fits well with Ireland's rich tradition of poetry and performance. Many famous novelists, poets and playwrights lived in Ireland, including James Joyce, Seamus Heaney and

Oscar Wilde. Cara enjoys poetry and arts and crafts, and hopes to study at Dublin's School of Creative Arts. "Irish people are very creative, we make glass, ceramics, music, all sorts of things!" Cara lives in a flat with her parents near the middle of Dublin. Cara's dad designs furniture and her mum is a software developer for Amazon. Amazon is one of the many international companies attracted to Ireland because the government doesn't ask businesses for as much money, called tax, as other countries. Cara also showed us where the famous Irish beer, Guinness, is brewed, which started back in 1759!

We say goodbye to Cara and Dublin, and explore more of the surrounding province, which is called Leinster. Ireland's four provinces, based on the boundaries of ancient kingdoms, are Ulster in the north, which we have already visited, Leinster in the east, Munster in the south and Connacht in the west. The country's major airport is at Dublin, but the east coast has several sea ports for goods and passengers travelling to and from Britain, France and other European countries. South of Dublin are the Wicklow Moun-

AMAZON OFFICES ARE IN DUBLIN

tains of County Wicklow, whose rounded granite peaks and wooded valleys are home to red squirrels, Irish hares and pine martens, which are all quite rare and hard to see in the British Isles. The Irish name for a pine marten, 'cat crainn', means 'tree cat' which seems to describe them pretty well!

Further inland are low-lying counties such as Westmeath, Laois and Offaly. They are known for their wetlands, and are popular with people who enjoy fishing and watersports. The vast peat bogs of central Ireland provide a home for many different plants and animals, and they even hide the remains of giant deer that went extinct thousands of years ago. So many fossils from this ancient creature have been preserved in Irish peat that it has become known as the Irish Elk, and their immense antlers can now be found decorating the dining halls of many Irish castles. The western border of the Leinster province is the great River Shannon, which flows slowly through central Ireland on its journey to the sea.

HIKING TRAIL IN THE WICKLOW MOUNTAINS

Republic of Ireland

PART II

THE RIVER SHANNON, named after a mythical Celtic goddess, is the largest river in Ireland. In fact, the Shannon is the longest river in the whole of the British Isles, as it is four miles longer than Britain's River Severn. It follows a slow and shallow course in a south and westerly direction through the middle of Ireland. It reaches the small, ancient city in southwest Ireland, called Limerick, which, by the way, has nothing to do with the limerick type of poem! Here, the Shannon flows past fine Georgian houses and museums, the bustling Milk Market and the medieval King John's Castle. The long Shannon estuary then leads out to the Atlantic Ocean, and if we were here in summer, we might see bottlenose dolphins and their calves swimming and playing in the water.

The source of the River Shannon is far away at the Shannon Pot in County Cavan in the northern province of Ulster. Three of Ulster's nine counties, Cavan, Monaghan and Donegal, are in the Republic of Ireland, while the other six form Northern Ireland. The Wild Atlantic Way is a coastal route which follows

the rough and rugged Atlantic shoreline of western Ireland. It starts at Malin Head in Donegal, in the far north of Ireland, and continues down through the provinces of Connacht and Munster, to Mizen Head in the south. Looking out to sea, there is nothing but 2,000 miles of untamed Atlantic Ocean. We can imagine how the wind and waves build up and up, and then crash ferociously into the rocks, cliffs and beaches of the shore! The spectacular and varied coastline, in many places indented like a zigzag, has wrecked many ships, but has also inspired artists and provided hours of exhilaration for surfers.

Locals recommend visiting the beautiful Cliffs of Moher in County Clare, which is roughly half-way up the west coast. The cliffs, which are rich in fossils, are made of layers of sandstone, mudstone and shale, and thousands of seabirds from razorbills to puffins build their nests here every year. Nearby we can find the wide Burren area of rocky limestone, which is grazed by cows in the winter and covered in colourful wildflowers in the summer. Underground is Doolin Cave, whose roof has the longest stalactite in Europe, taller than a giraffe! Doolin village is a hub of traditional music, where bands play folk tunes on the accordion and fiddle. From here we could hop on a boat to the Aran Islands, which are famous for their knitted jumpers, as well as their ancient forts and churches. Further up the coast, in County Donegal, are the much higher cliffs at Slieve League, which means 'grey mountain.' These 'megacliffs' tower higher than 600m above the Atlantic waves, which makes them three times higher than the Cliffs of Moher, and six times as high as the White Cliffs of Dover in England!

Doolin Caves with the Great Stalactite

Another important mountain is Croagh Patrick, the 'holy mountain', in County Mayo. Croagh Patrick is almost a perfect pyramid, made of glistening quartzite and occasional seams of gold. Ireland's patron saint, St Patrick, was the first to bring Christianity to the people of Ireland and he is said to have fasted on this mountain for forty days. Now, every year, thousands of people climb it as pilgrims, some with bare feet! Legend has it that

St Patrick used the shamrock, a plant whose one leaf is split into three parts, to explain the Christian belief about the Trinity, that there is one God in three persons, Father, Son and Holy Spirit. The shamrock has become a symbol of Ireland, as have Celtic crosses and the Celtic harp, which was played by court musicians for Irish chieftains and kings a thousand years ago.

In the south-west of Ireland is the province of Munster. A large valley known as the Golden Vale in County Tipperary is rich with fertile farmland. Fruit farms flourish and local cheeses are sold in the market towns and further afield. Further south, in County Cork, we can find rugged mountains and wild coasts. Ireland's second largest city, Cork, sits here beside the south coast. Cork has one of the largest natural harbours in the world and a busy port. It is also a hub of business and industry, and many people are employed making medicines for Pfizer, computer software for Apple and sweets like Tic Tacs.

Nearby, County Kerry is renowned for its beautiful and

KERRYGOLD BUTTER LEAVING THE FACTORY

unspoilt places. Here we find Ireland's tallest mountain, Carrauntoohil, and Ireland's most westerly point, the Dingle peninsula. These remote regions in the west of Ireland are the strongholds of traditional culture and folklore. Here, tales are told of fairies and leprechauns, and the Irish language, a form of Gaelic, is spoken by many. Indeed, these Irish-speaking places are called 'Gaeltacht' and school students from other parts of Ireland, like Cara from Dublin, sometimes visit for a few weeks in the summer. They stay in a local home to learn Irish and enjoy traditional music, food and literature. Corned beef and soda bread might be on the menu, along with colcannon, which is a stew made of cabbage and mashed potato. Potatoes are a favourite food across Ireland, though they are also sadly linked to a terrible Potato Famine, when the crop rotted in the 1840s. This famine led to millions of Irish people starving or moving away to North America. Now, all over the world, people with surnames such as O'Brien, O'Connor, Kennedy or Murphy can trace their family trees back to their Irish ancestors. Some even make the journey back to Ireland, to meet up with long-lost cousins and rediscover their roots in the Emerald Isle.

Conclusion

WHAT A LOT of things we have seen and discovered in our tour of the British Isles! We have seen the beautiful landscape, from steep mountains and rolling hills to flat fenland and peaty bogs. We have explored the long coastline, from sheltered bays and sand banks to whirlpools and rugged cliffs. We have heard about the mild, rainy climate, the long meandering rivers and the land's natural resources. I wonder which of these places you would like to visit in real life?

Geography is about the way places shape the lives of the people who live there: the jobs they do, the kind of towns they live in and the things they like to do for fun. In the British Isles we have seen that the natural landscape has affected the location of towns and factories, and the types of farming and hobbies that are possible. Over the centuries, it has also inspired art and stories, shaped cultural traditions and music, and even the languages that are spoken. Can you imagine how different the British Isles would have been if they had a hot, dry climate, or if the Scottish Highlands had no mountains, or if Great Britain and Ireland were joined together?

We have also seen some ways that people themselves shape

the places where they live. We have heard of landscapes transformed by people who built castles and motorways, cities and reservoirs, and who drained all the water from the fens. These islands are filled with evidence of the people's history and culture, their beliefs and inventions, and the ways they have moved around and shared ideas. Can you imagine how different the British Isles would have been if nobody lived here at all?

The history of the British Isles is the story of people making the most of their opportunities. They benefited from their location in the world, as islanders at the edge of a continent. When Europeans discovered the Americas, the British Isles were well placed to have links in both directions, both east and west. We have also seen how their culture of seafaring and shipbuilding, exploration and trade contributed to Britain becoming a powerful country with a large empire, for better or worse. Britain was also the first country in the world to have an Industrial Revolution. This was made possible because there was plenty of coal and iron ore in the ground and the people's

Christian religion encouraged them to find out about nature, God's creation. They made progress in science and technology, making machines that could quickly weave cotton and wool, and power steam trains and ships. For many years the British Isles were the workshop of the world, making goods that were sent by ship from dozens of ports to many other countries. Can you imagine how different the British Isles would have been if the people had not had the Industrial Revolution, or if they had been afraid of the sea and never travelled to other countries?

As the centuries have gone by, there have been many changes both to the landscape and people's way of life. In some ways the physical landscape matters less than it once did. In the past, you would have eaten the food that could be grown nearby, and too much rain and a bad harvest meant you would go hungry. You would never have seen bananas, pasta or chocolate. Now that we have better technology and transport, food and other goods can quickly and easily be moved between countries, by plane and ship, all year round. Oil is transported in huge tanker ships and gas is piped under the sea. Countries like China are now the workshops of the world, whereas British and Irish people are more likely to work in desk jobs, providing services like healthcare, finance and research. Their location in between Europe and America, East and West, is still very useful, and there are many international connections. London is one of the world's major financial centres. British banks lend money all over the world and insurance companies protect people from losing money in fires or earthquakes. Scientists produce new medicines for the world, engineers build bridges in other countries, overseas students study in the universities and foreign tourists visit the historical and cultural sights. Can you imagine never eating bananas, pasta or chocolate, and never meeting anyone from other countries?

People from different countries are far more connected with each other now than in the past. At one time most people would have lived their whole lives in one place, farming or mining or working in some other local industry. Now, people travel to other countries to go on holiday, to work, to trade or to move house. Communities need to learn to get along with people from different backgrounds, while still remembering and celebrating their own history and culture. We make friends from other places, we see different countries on the television and internet, and it is quicker and cheaper than ever to actually go there ourselves. All this travel and technology also creates its own problems, though. Petrol driven cars and planes cause air pollution, and plastic packaging, designed to keep food fresh on long journeys, can end up in the sea. Electricity can now be made from water, wind, nuclear power and the sun, and perhaps new and better technology will be developed soon. People are also learning to think about how they can reduce, reuse and recycle the things they buy, to create less waste. Can you imagine any other, better ways of creating energy or protecting the environment?

Some parts of the British Isles have very few people living there, but many other parts are becoming built up and crowded. Better technology has led to better food and medicine, so people generally live longer. Also, immigration, where people move from other countries, has continued. All these extra people need places to live, and we often prefer to live in houses with gardens, which take more space than flats or apartments.

Towns and cities have got bigger, new roads and railways are being built and many more houses are still needed. This means it is increasingly important to look after the countryside and to design new towns, streets and houses that will be pleasant places to live. Beautiful and unspoilt landscapes have become important for tourism, because people like to visit the countryside and relax. This creates lots of jobs for people living in the remoter parts of the British Isles, for example in hotels and cafes, though some are only busy in the summer. Green belts and national parks have been created in many places to conserve the landscape and wildlife, protect dark skies to keep them free from bright city lights, and preserve the distinctive character of local villages. Do you prefer busy places or quiet places?

Perhaps you have more questions about the British Isles. Perhaps one day you will cycle Ireland's Wild Atlantic Way or clamber over the Giant's Causeway. Perhaps you will climb to the top of Ben Nevis or explore the caves of the Peak District. Perhaps you will watch the tall ships set sail from Portsmouth Harbour or learn to make Welsh cakes in Cardiff. Perhaps there are things about the traditions of these islands that you think should be kept for the future. Perhaps there are things that you hope will change. Perhaps you will help to protect the natural landscape or to develop environmentally-friendly transport. Perhaps you can imagine what the British Isles will be like in ten, a hundred, or a thousand years' time. Perhaps you can help them to get better and better.